# JOB

## INTO THE FIRE,
## OUT OF THE ASHES

TONY & JAN CARTLEDGE

Annual
Bible
Study

*Study Guide*

SMYTH&HELWYS
PUBLISHING INCORPORATED · MACON GEORGIA

# CONTENTS

**Annual Bible Study**

**Cecil P. Staton, Jr.**
President & CEO

**Lex Horton**
Publisher / Executive Vice
President

**P. Keith Gammons**
Vice President, Production

**Mark K. McElroy**
Senior Editor

**Leslie Andres**
Editor

**Kelley F. Land**
Assistant Editor

**Betsy Butler**
Associate Editor

**Barclay Burns**
**Wesley Crook**
**Dave Jones**
Graphic Design

**Cover art**
(Credit: *Job and Friends*,
Gustave Doré)

Sidebar material has been adapted
from Samuel Balentine, *Job*,
Smyth & Helwys Bible Commentary
(Macon GA: Smyth & Helwys, 2006).

1-800-747-3016 (USA)
1-800-568-1248 (Canada)

SMYTH&HELWYS
PUBLISHING INCORPORATED · MACON, GEORGIA
WWW.HELWYS.COM

# ACKNOWLEDGMENTS

The writing of any work is the culmination of much that goes before. We are grateful to those who have loved us, educated us, and encouraged us. When we sat on the ash heap with Job following the death of our daughter, Bethany, in 1994, we were blessed by a host of friends who cared for us with tender compassion and none of the judgment that Job experienced from his "comforters." In reliving some of those moments while writing these lessons, we were reminded of how grateful we are.

Our brothers and sisters of HomeStar Fellowship, the family of faith that we call home, were faithful encouragers and contributed helpful feedback as we worked through these studies with them.

We offer special appreciation to our son, Samuel, who has patiently endured while one or the other of his parents was distracted with the writing of these words.

And, as we followed Job through his painful struggle for answers, we joined him in quiet amazement when considering the wonder of a God who may not give the answers we seek but is always present in ways beyond our imagining.

Jan and Tony Cartledge

# PREFACE

"You have heard of the patience of Job," said one New Testament writer (Jas 5:11). But have you heard of his *im*patience? One who reads beyond the first two chapters of the book of Job will soon learn that Job's famed patience lasted barely a week. Shortly after suffering unspeakable tragedies, Job spoke surprisingly impassive words of acceptance and trust in God in the face of loss. After seven days of suffering in silence, however, Job filled the air with complaints and accusations toward the God who had repaid his righteousness with ravaging. That side of Job is less familiar but far more important for helping us understand the book's message.

The book of Job is not about patience but about theology, and in particular, about *theodicy*. Theology is an attempt to study and learn about God. Theodicy focuses on the attempt to understand divine justice, or the apparent lack of it.

All people who live long enough will experience pain and suffering at some point, unexpected sorrows that lead them to join Job in questioning whether God is playing fair.

Questions come easily; answers are hard. Studying the sorrowful story of Job requires us to enter a dark world that is sometimes

**Job**

Jusepe de Ribera (1591–1652). *Job*. Galleria Nazionale, Parma, Italy. (Credit: Scala/Art Resource, NY)

painfully like our own, with the exception that few modern readers can claim Job's level of personal piety or have suffered comparable losses. We may be more likely than Job to suspect that we may indeed deserve our fate, while Job was certain of his innocence. Sometimes, like Job, the lesson we learn may be that there are no clear answers or that we have been asking the wrong questions.

The book of Job recounts a dark and dangerous journey toward unseen insights that challenge both human assumptions and traditional theological beliefs. Those who dare to enter Job's world may discover that their own world—or view of the world—has changed in surprising ways. In the end, however, those who stick with the ancient sufferer may discover spiritual depths they had not previously imagined.

# JOB'S INNOCENT AFFLICTION

### Focal text: 1:1–2:13

## INTRODUCTION

Before digging into the text of Job's story, it is important to grasp a basic understanding of how Job fits into the literary context of the Bible as well as the cultural context of the ancient Near East.

### Job in Context

The Bible includes many types of literature, ranging from history and legal codes to prophecies and love songs. The book of Job belongs to a category that is often called "Wisdom literature." Like the books of Proverbs and Ecclesiastes, it has a distinctly didactic purpose.

Wisdom traditions were not unique to the Hebrews, however, nor were the kind of questions asked by the book of Job. Some of the most intriguing documents from ancient Mesopotamia and Egypt are the work of thoughtful sages who sought to understand and to teach. Wisdom literature takes many forms, including proverbs, riddles, practical advice, and even philosophical ponderings.

The biblical book most readily recognized was Wisdom literature is the book of Proverbs, which contains several collections of sensible maxims for a prudent and successful life. Proverbs such as these were used mainly for the education of young men.

Aphorisms are helpful, but the ancients understood that the "standard wisdom" of a proverb doesn't always pan out. To illustrate with a popular American proverb, "no pain, no gain" is generally true, but not always. Sometimes there is pain without much gain. Sometimes people are born to great wealth, a gain that requires no pain.

The books of Job and Ecclesiastes could be called "speculative wisdom," for they call traditional teachings into question. Ancient texts from the Sumerian, Babylonian, and Egyptian civilizations raised similar questions (for the curious, the Teacher's Guide for this study includes specific examples). The Hebrews, like their ancient neighbors, sought answers to life's hard questions.

Since the people of Israel spent considerable time in both Egypt and Mesopotamia, it should come as no surprise that Israel's Wisdom literature reflects cross-cultural influences. Note, for example, that even Job is not depicted as an Israelite, but as a resident of "Uz," an unknown location somewhere east of the Jordan, perhaps in Edom.

## Literary Development

The story of Job is set in the ancient past, long before Israel existed. The only other Old Testament reference to Job is in Ezekiel 14:14, which puts Job in the company of Noah and possibly the Ugaritic hero Dan-el, who was famous in Canaanite legend for his justice and wisdom.

While the book may reflect ancient traditions, it probably was not written until the post-exilic period (fourth through fifth centuries BC), when the surprisingly hard life of returning exiles raised hard questions about what one could expect of God. Books like Ezra and Nehemiah show how the Israelites joyfully returned from exile to resettle the promised land, but found Jerusalem ruined and the surrounding countryside occupied by hostile peoples. Some wondered if God had betrayed them.

Portions of the text include words borrowed from the Aramaic and Arabic languages that gained wider use in the post-exilic period, suggesting that the book did not reach its final form until the fifth century BC at the earliest.

The story of Job may have been written in stages. It begins with a prologue (1:1–2:13) and ends with an epilogue (42:7-17), both in prose, that tell the story of a righteous man who lost everything through a divine wager far beyond his control, but who proved himself true despite horrific suffering and saw his fortunes restored in double measure. The prose story could stand alone, and some scholars regard this as the oldest part of the book into which lengthy poetic dialogues were later inserted.

The massive core of the book is a series of conversations between Job and three friends (chs. 3–31) into which an anonymous poem on the elusiveness of wisdom has been inserted (ch. 28). This is followed by a series of speeches by a self-important visitor named Elihu (chs. 32–37) and a two-part dialogue between God (who does most of the talking) and a chastened Job (38:1–42:6). These may have been added at different times as the book developed.

## Theological Purpose

The book of Job, like other Wisdom literature, depends strongly on a theology of creation and has little to say about the salvation history that runs through much of the Old Testament. The reader will notice many references to God's creation of light, of the world, and of living things.

Job is not portrayed as a Jew, but he is described as one who worshiped Yahweh (God's personal name, usually translated as "LORD"). Job also observed sacrifices and other customs similar to those of the later Hebrews. Most importantly, Job's story is written from the traditional belief that obedience to God results in blessings, while those who rebel and sin are cursed with punishments. This theology is clearly taught in Deuteronomy, with Deuteronomy 28 being a prime example of the belief that God rewards righteousness and punishes evil.

Often, however, good people suffer and the wicked prosper. Honest questioners like the author(s) of Job dared to ask the same hard questions we may ponder: Why do the innocent suffer? Why do the promises fail? Why does God sometimes seem more capricious than compassionate?

In the end, the book reaches no firm conclusion and offers no final answer beyond the suggestion that Job had been asking the wrong questions. God offers no guarantees, no explanations, and no excuses. What God does offer is the assurance of divine presence despite human darkness, an impressive self-revelation that leads Job to conclude, "Now my eye sees you" (42:5).

# STUDY APPROACH

Our all-too-brief study of Job is divided into four sessions. This introductory session will go on to discuss the prologue (1:1–2:13), the familiar part of the book that describes how a righteous man came to lose everything. The second session deals with Job's bitter lament (3:1-26) in which he has moved long past patience and wishes for death. In session 3, we'll look at excerpts from 4:1–14:22, the first of three lengthy cycles of dialogue between Job and his friends. The final session examines God's response to Job and its aftermath (38:1–42:17).

For those who wish to see the larger context, here is a suggested outline of the entire book:

I. Prologue: A heavenly wager played out on earth: 1:1–2:13
    A. Job: the earth's most righteous man (1:1-5)
    B. God and the accuser wager on Job's integrity (1:6-12)
    C. Job is ruined but faithful (1:13-22)
    D. God's second wager, with more personal stakes (2:1-6)
    E. Job loses his health but holds fast his integrity (2:7-10)
    F. Job's friends honor him with silence (2:11-13)
II. Job and his friends seek understanding: 3:1–31:40
    A. Job's lament (3:1-26)
    B. Cycles of speech and response (4:1–27:23)
        1. The first cycle (4:1–14:22)
            a. Eliphaz speaks (4:1–5:27) and Job responds (6:1–7:21)
            b. Bildad speaks (8:1-22) and Job responds (9:1–10:22)
            c. Zophar speaks (11:1-20) and Job responds (12:1–14:22)
        2. The second cycle (15:1–21:34)
            a. Eliphaz speaks (15:1-35) and Job responds (16:1–17:16)
            b. Bildad speaks (18:1-21) and Job responds (19:1-29)
            c. Zophar speaks (20:1-29) and Job responds (21:1-34)
        3. The third cycle (22:1–27:23)
            a. Eliphaz speaks (22:1-30) and Job responds (23:1–24:25)
            b. Bildad speaks (25:1-6) and Job responds (26:1–27:23)
            c. (Nothing is attributed to Zophar in this cycle)
    C. A hymn to elusive wisdom (28:1-28)
    D. Job's closing arguments (29:1–31:40)
    E. Elihu's speeches claim to have the answer (32:1–37:24)
III. Job meets his maker: 38:1–42:6
    A. God speaks from a whirlwind (38:1–40:2) and Job is silent (40:3-5)
    B. God speaks again (40:6–41:34) and Job understands (42:1-6)
IV. Epilogue: Job's fortunes are restored: 42:7-17

# BIBLICAL BACKGROUND

Stop any person on the street and ask them what they know about the biblical Job. If they know anything at all, it will probably come from the first two chapters, the familiar story of how God and an angelic accuser make a bet on whether Job will remain faithful if the accuser takes away his family, his property, and his health. That limited knowledge fails to recognize the deep and important question addressed by the book, namely, "Why do I serve God?"

While we think of Job as a story, most of the book is composed of poetry— no less than thirty-nine of the forty-two chapters. Most of it consists of poetic dialogues between Job and his "comforters," or between Job and God. The first two chapters and most of the last chapter (42:7-17) are written in prose. These narrative sections bracket the large, poetic middle section like the covers of a book.

The prose frame, divided into a prologue and epilogue, appears to be the oldest part of the book. Why do we say this? One reason is that the vocabulary, including the names used for God, is characteristic of earlier writings. The narrative sections commonly refer to God as "Yahweh," the Hebrews' personal name for God (23 times), with some uses of the more generic "Elohim" (11 times).

"Yahweh" is the Hebrew form of the more familiar name "Jehovah," which is based on an early misunderstanding of how the divine name YHWH should be pronounced. Here's what happened: the Hebrew Bible was written with consonants only. Vowels, in the form of diacritical marks called "vowel points," were added later. While English transliterates the Hebrew letters *yod* and *waw* as Y and W, Germans use J and V. That, combined with a failure to recognize that the scribes had respectfully pointed the name *yhwh* (*jhvh* to Germans) with the vowels for *'elohim*, led to the hybrid name "Jehovah," which came into English use from German.

The name "Yahweh" appears more frequently in older literature. In later periods, the Hebrews thought of God as more distant and began to shy away from using God's personal name. The poetic sections of Job seem to reflect this later usage. They are more inclined to refer to God with titles like "El" (55 times), "Eloah" (41 times), and "Shaddai" (31 times).

The first two chapters of Job begin with an introduction of Job (1:1-5) and end with the introduction of his friends (2:11-13). In between, the story describes two tests in which God and the "*šāṭān*" discuss Job's exemplary faith and wager on whether Job would remain faithful if his blessings were removed (1:6-22; 2:1-10).

## Job, the Righteous—1:1-5

The story of Job is told like a folk tale. As familiar tales begin with "Once upon a time," Job's story begins with "A man there was in the land of Uz, whose name was Job."

As in folk tales, the account is less than specific about Job's homeland of "Uz." The location of Uz is uncertain. It was presumably not in Israel; otherwise it would not be preceded by "the land of." Places were sometimes named after their founding citizen, and biblical genealogies list several men named "Uz" (Gen 10:23; 22:21; 36:2; 1 Chr 1:17, 42). The first listed is the son of Aram (Gen 10:23), whose descendants reportedly lived north and east of Palestine. "The kings of the land of Uz" are mentioned in Jeremiah 25:20, but the location of Uz is not given. Our best clue is found in Lamentations 4:21, which addresses the "daughter of Edom, you that live in the land of Uz." This suggests that Uz was located in the general area known as Edom, which was south of the Dead Sea and largely east of Israel, the extreme southern part of what is now the Hashemite Kingdom of Jordan.

The meaning of Job's name is as mysterious as the location of his home. In Hebrew, it is "*'iyyôb*," which may be derived from a verb that means "to hate." Some suggest it might mean something like "the hated one" or "the persecuted one." Job's name may have no particular significance, however.

While the meaning of Job's name is uncertain, there is no question that the author wants us to understand that Job is a righteous man, innocent of any wrongdoing that might call for divine punishment.

Job has been famously faithful (1:1), which presumably explains why he has also been blessed with ten children (1:2) and massive livestock holdings (1:3). Job, indeed, is so wealthy that the author calls him "the greatest of all the people of the East."

Job was not only the wealthiest, but also so pious that he looked after his children's spiritual health in addition to his own. Following special feast days when his children and their families celebrated together (1:4)—probably on each son's birthday—Job would "sanctify them" and offer burnt offerings for each of them, just in case they had sinned or "cursed God in their hearts" (1:5).

"This is what Job always did" is the author's way of indicating that Job's acts of sacrifice and sanctification were the consistent habits of a conscientious, blameless man. Even Yahweh recognized that there was "no one like him on the earth" (1:8).

## Job's First Test—1:6-22

Job's unexpected downfall did not begin on earth, but in heaven, where "the heavenly beings"—literally, "the sons of God"—came to present themselves before Yahweh. The Hebrews believed that angelic beings occasionally gathered for decision-making meetings with God (see, for example, Pss 58 and 82). Israel's neighbors had similar ideas. In both Canaanite and Mesopotamian religion, it was believed that a heavenly council met each New Year's Day to determine the fate of the earth's inhabitants for the coming year.

No occasion is given for the meeting of Yahweh's divine council described in Job 1, but the narrator carefully notes that the "*śāṭān*" was among the "sons of God" who attended. This particular character is commonly misunderstood, and his name is generally mistranslated, even by the NRSV. The "*śāṭān*" as described in the book of Job is pointedly not the Satan or "devil" described in later Christian theology. He is neither evil nor one who tempts others to do evil, but is clearly identified as one of the "sons of God," a member of the divine council who went to and fro to do Yahweh's bidding.

Wherever this character appears in Job, he is identified by his title rather than by a personal name: *haśśāṭān* is a combination of two words: "the" (ha) and "accuser" or "adversary" (*śāṭān*, pronounced "sah-TAHN"). In Job, the *śāṭān* plays the role of a

**Satan Going Forth from the Presence of the Lord**

William Blake (1757-1827). *Satan Going Forth from the Presence of the Lord*. 1823-1825. Engraving from Blake's *Illustrations of the Book of Job*.

heavenly district attorney, roaming the earth in search of sinners who deserve a dose of divine justice.

The accuser suggests that Yahweh's pride in Job's faithful and upright lifestyle (1:8) is misplaced. Indeed, the *śāṭān* suggests that Job's reverent service to God is purely selfish. He asks, "Does Job fear God for nothing?" This question is at the heart of Job 1–2.

The accuser charges that if Job's fortunes were lost, he would curse God soon enough. In 1:10-11, Job shows great concern that his children not curse God. Will he turn about and curse God himself if his blessings are lost?

The amazing thing about the chapter is that Yahweh accepts the accuser's challenge. In effect, the *śāṭān's* challenge puts God in a difficult position. If Yahweh refuses to take the bet, the accuser could suggest that God is afraid of the possibility that Job's faith might be selfishly motivated. If God agrees to the wager, Job will suffer without cause: there is no easy way out.

In the end, Yahweh accepts the wager, believing that Job will remain faithful even in the face of pain and loss. While the accuser bets that suffering will turn Job's praise to cursing, Yahweh bets that Job will be true.

Try to imagine what the experience might have been like from Job's perspective. In a world where wealth was measured by cattle and servants, Job owned 7,000 sheep and 3,000 camels, 500 yoke of oxen and just as many donkeys, along with sufficient servants to take care of them so that Job could devote his own time to being a model of righteousness.

It was late at night. Perhaps he and his wife were already in bed when a field hand with a nasty wound on his head and blood running down the side of his face came running to his house, banging on the door.

"Master Job!" he cried. "Master Job! We were out in the fields. All of the oxen were plowing as you directed. All of the donkeys were grazing in their pasture. Suddenly we were surrounded. The Sabeans came silently from the south. They swept down upon us from the hills with their wicked swords. They stole every one of your oxen and all of the donkeys. They slaughtered your servants! They knocked me unconscious and thought I was dead. I woke up and realized I was the only survivor, so I came to tell you. . . ."

You wouldn't want to be that field hand, nor would you want to be the wild-eyed shepherd who came panting to the door before the field hand could finish his story.

"Master Job! Master Job! You won't believe what happened, but I swear it is true! Your servants were out in the distant fields, watching the sheep as you directed us. Suddenly the sky darkened and a storm from the west swept over us. We huddled the sheep together for warmth, but we were all soaked to the skin. Then the lightning began! Strong bolts of fire began striking right in the middle of the flock. Every sheep you own was killed, and all of the servants. I was coming back for help when I turned and saw it happen. I am the only survivor!"

You wouldn't want to be Job or his field hand or his shepherd, but you wouldn't want to be his lead camel-driver, either. He also came bolting in while his predecessor was still speaking, and he looked even worse than the other two.

"Master Job! Master Job! We took the camels out for pasture as you directed, and we were guarding them carefully against raiders. But we were attacked by a whole division of the Chaldean army! They came from the north, divided into three companies, and swarmed all over us. They drew their swords and killed all of your servants, then stole all of your camels. Only I escaped, and I have come to take my punishment for failing you."

You wouldn't want to be Job or his field hand or his shepherd or his camel-driver. But you really wouldn't want to be the young maid who came rushing in from the rain and stumbled over the kneeling camel-driver. She was drenched with rain, but that did not hide her tears.

"Master Job! Master Job! All your sons and daughters were feasting together in your oldest son's house. There was a noise so loud we couldn't hear each other. We looked out and saw a dark cloud coming toward us. A great wind from the east slammed into the house. The walls shook, and then they fell, and part of them blew away. I hid under the kitchen table, and when I came out, I found them all dead. Every one! I alone have survived to tell you!" (1:13-19)

In the space of a single night, everything was gone. Those who were around Job moaned and cried out at the unfairness of it all. We can imagine that Job's wife may have alternated between sobs and screams and trying to catch her breath and comprehend the depth of their loss. Job was affected also, but the text suggests that he took it much more calmly. He tore his robe according to custom and shaved his head as a sign of mourning, and he fell on the ground before God and prayed, but very politely. Then he got up and made an announcement: "I was naked when I came from my mother's womb," he said, "and I'll be naked when I die. The LORD gave, and the LORD has taken away. Blessed be the name of the LORD" (1:20-21).

Job's response to the multiplied disasters is mind-boggling. One could hardly expect Job to sing a hymn of praise; the amazing thing is that he did not pronounce an angry curse. Despite his suffering, however, Job did not curse, but offered a blessing! Though he had been reduced to poverty and rendered childless, and though he acknowledged that God was responsible for his loss, Job yet managed to say "blessed be the name of the LORD" (1:21—"LORD" spelled in small caps indicates the divine name "Yahweh").

"Naked I came from my mother's womb, and naked shall I return there" begins with a literal statement and ends with a metaphor. Job does not imagine that he will strip off his clothing and reenter his dead mother's womb at the time of death ("naked shall I return there"), but he recognizes that those who die take nothing with them when they return to the earth. Many years later, the Apostle Paul would make the same point to Timothy: "for we brought nothing into the world, so that we can take nothing out of it" (1 Tim 6:7).

Job's statement assigns no blame, but acknowledges that God has the right and power both to give and to take away. To ensure that the reader does not miss the point, the narrator adds, "In all this Job did not sin or charge God with wrongdoing" (1:22).

## Job's Second Test—2:1-10

The account of Job's second test begins precisely as the first, with the heavenly beings (literally, "sons of God") attending upon Yahweh in a divine council meeting. Those present include the accuser, who reports on what he has seen while traversing the earth and observing the behavior of humankind (2:1-2). Again Yahweh points with pride to Job as "a blameless and upright man who fears God and turns away from evil," noting with satisfaction that "He still persists in his integrity, although you incited me against him, to destroy him for no reason" (2:3).

The reader may find it surprising that Yahweh openly admits to having been "incited" against Job "for no reason." The Hebrew word *hinnam*, translated here as "for no reason," is the same word used in 1:9, where the accuser asks, "Does Job fear God for nothing?"

The *śāṭān* is unconvinced, however. He insists that Job's faith would crumble if calamity touched his own skin, if he faced the physical equivalent of his financial and family losses (2:4-5). Yahweh recognizes that Job is "blameless" and deserves no suffering, but agrees to a second wager on whether Job would turn against Yahweh if his health were lost (2:6). Yahweh's continued willingness to let Job suffer for the sake of divine pride may lead the reader to wonder if it is God, rather than Job, who is being tested.

With God's permission to take all but Job's last breath, the accuser wastes no time in striking again. Job's troubles did not come with the suddenness of his family and property losses, but he was soon stricken with a disease that covered his body with "loathsome sores" (2:7), making his life utterly miserable and rendering him ritually unclean. Some writers have gone to great lengths to try to diagnose Job's specific condition, with suggestions ranging from leprosy to elephantiasis to malignant ulcers. We don't really need a specific diagnosis, however; what matters is that the condition brought constant misery to Job and made his presence repulsive.

Not wishing to impose his uncleanness upon others, Job voluntarily retreated to the family trash heap, where ashes from the cooking fire were piled with broken pottery and other household garbage (2:8).

While Job is the focus of the story, one must remember that Job's wife—who is not named—has shared in his suffering. Indeed, her pain over the loss of the children could have been sharper and deeper than Job's, and the loss of the family's wealth would affect her no less than Job. Only at the point of Job's physical affliction did her experience part from his, though that does not mean she escaped the suffering: it is not easy to watch a loved one experience pain.

**Job and His Wife**

Georges de La Tour (1593–1652). *Job and His Wife*. Early 1630s. Musee Departemental des Vosges, Epinal, France. (Credit: Erich Lessing/Art Resource, NY)

In the face of Job's withering disease, his wife appears to have broken with the strain. Finding it hard to see Job suffer, and perhaps feeling personal anger toward God, she urged Job to get it over with, to curse God and die (2:9). Though his wife challenged Job's integrity, he remained firm in his convictions and professed a belief that one's attitude toward God should not be dependent on material or physical blessings: "Shall we receive the good at the hand of God, and not receive the bad?" (2:10a).

Job's composure in the face of trial is hard to imagine. Yet, the narrator again reaffirms Job's steadfastness in avoiding sin despite the *śāṭān*'s extreme attempts to provoke him: "In all this Job did not sin with his lips" (2:10b).

## Job's Friends Arrive—2:11-13

The final verses of chapter 2 serve as a transition to the arrival of Job's friends. There are no more debates in the heavenly council and no further appearances of the *śāṭān*: the remainder of Job's story takes place on the earth. Until God speaks from the whirlwind in Job 38, the search for understanding will come entirely through dialogues between Job and his visitors.

The narrative says nothing about how Job's friends learned of his trials, but provides enough information to suggest that they also lived in the East. Eliphaz (whose name means "my god is fine gold") is from Teman, known to be in northern Edom (Amos 1:12; Jer 49:20; Ezek 25:13). Bildad, whose name might mean "beloved of Bel" or "son of Hadad," is called "the Shuhite," a reference to the region of Shuah. The area may have been named after Shuah, a son of Abraham and Keturah, who was sent with his brothers to live away from Isaac "in the East country." Zophar's provenance is as mysterious as his name, which is otherwise unknown and may be related to identical roots that can mean "bird" or "he-goat."

When they first arrived, the men behaved as true friends. They hardly recognized the disfigured man in the ashes as Job: they had known him as the "greatest man in the east," but now they saw that his suffering was "very great." Job had gone from the top of the world to the bottom. The men did what true friends do when consoling one who has faced tragedy: they sat in the ashes with him. Recognizing that the time for words was not yet, they sat in silence for seven days, presumably fasting and comforting Job through the gift of their presence and their willingness to share his suffering.

## THEOLOGICAL THEMES: THE PROVIDENCE— AND FREEDOM—OF GOD

The book of Job raises questions about the providence of God. Job suffers greatly but has no idea that his earthly loss results from a heavenly wager and that Yahweh has acknowledged his suffering is undeserved.

Is this the way God works? Could a lesser being truly incite God to smite an innocent man in order to prove a point? Some readers find encouragement in the thought that God cares about the thoughts of created beings (including humans), and might be influenced by them. God's response to the accuser's challenge, however, strikes other readers as unworthy of God. Even Job's friends, in later chapters, put all the blame on Job and did not imagine that his suffering might have resulted from a divine dare. They assumed that God was punishing Job for some sin, in keeping with their traditional beliefs.

Job never wavered from his declaration of innocence, and the narrator supports his claim to integrity. Even Yahweh affirmed that Job was "blameless and upright." Nevertheless, he suffered the fate one would expect of the wicked. Why? What do we learn from this discomforting story?

One lesson, repeated in a variety of ways, is that God is sovereign and cannot be limited to the theological boxes humans construct. A god who is truly God must act independently and freely, not necessarily subject to what humans think God must do.

Near the end of C. S. Lewis's familiar *The Lion, the Witch, and the Wardrobe*, Mr. Beaver speaks to the children who have come into Narnia and tries to explain something about the nature of the great Aslan, an obvious Christ figure. "He is not a tame lion," Beaver says, a statement both simple and profound.

The reader of Job, if nothing else, will learn that Yahweh is not a tame God.

## LITERARY THEMES

An examination of the literary characteristics of the book of Job is valuable in pondering the heavy questions it raises. Should we interpret the book literally, or read it as a parable?

One who interprets the book literally, believing that Job and his situation should be understood as historically accurate, is forced to accept the premise that God can be provoked into playing cruel games with human lives, smiting even the most righteous follower "for no reason" (2:13).

From this perspective, one might find evidence of God's sovereignty to act in ways that supersede human reason, but always for a reason. Since Job is ultimately restored, one might find support for the common belief that "everything happens for a reason." If that is the case, Job never discovers what that reason might be. He ultimately acknowledges God's supreme ability to do as God pleases, but he never understands why God chose him for an object lesson.

Readers should be aware that it is also possible to approach the story of Job as an extended parable, a fictional creation or expanded story through which the wisdom teachers of Israel sought to expand the minds of their students.

We have noted above that the book shows clear signs of development: an old prose narrative is expanded via the insertion of poetic dialogues in what appear to be at least two stages.

The book's obvious literary development, its similarity in theme to other ancient Near Eastern works, its ambiguous setting in an uncertain locale, and its folkloristic "there once was a man" beginning all support the idea that the book of Job is a literary creation, though it may be attached to a historical figure.

With this perspective, the reader is not required to assume that the author listened in on a heavenly council meeting, that a secretary took rapid notes on clay tablets as Job and his friends traded lengthy monologues on the meaning of suffering, or that a later scribe took it all down by divine dictation. Rather, one can recognize the possibility that the sages responsible for the story of Job were inspired to create a literary scenario for exploring important theological issues, even as a modern pastor may construct practical illustrations to help parishioners grapple with theological matters, while still honoring the Scripture as an authoritative guide for gaining glimpses of God.

## SPIRITUALITY AND MINISTRY THEMES

Several of the themes in Job raise universal questions. What should we expect out of life? What can we expect from God? Perhaps the central issue is the question of why we should worship God.

## What Can We Expect from God?

When Job is introduced, his life is idyllic, as if living in Eden. Job and his family have success in every endeavor. As the patriarch of his family, Job cares for his children in the same way God seems to be caring for him—providing for all their needs and even making efforts to protect them from harm. The prologue introduces us to a time of peace and prosperity when life is good, the kind of life we hope for.

No matter how upright we might be, however, evil may come. Job turned away from doing evil, yet evil came upon him, perhaps the ultimate example of the reality that bad things happen to good people. The author portrays Job as perfectly upright, yet he lost ten children, unnumbered grandchildren, and all his possessions in a single day.

Does God bring evil upon us, or allow evil to come, for divine purposes that we may or may not ever come to understand? Those who hold a Calvinistic understanding of divine sovereignty or predestination might answer in the affirmative. Some people believe that everything happens for a reason, that God controls every action and that every trial is sent for some purpose—perhaps as discipline for sin, or as a divinely designed lesson intended to strengthen the believer and prepare him or her for some future trial of greater severity.

A better approach for most situations, perhaps, is to recognize that evil is the natural consequence of human choice. Humans may choose to commit sin, to do wrong, and to hurt other people. As a result, both they and their victims suffer in a variety of ways. I (Tony) will never forget how I came to realize, some weeks after a drunk driver killed our young daughter in 1994, that Romans 6:23 ("the wages of sin is death") does not apply to the sinner alone.[1] Though we normally interpret that verse to mean that those who live in sin will earn eternal death, it is also true that one person's evil can lead to another person's earthly death.

I do not believe God caused Bethany's death in order to teach us a lesson, though we have learned many things. I do not believe God killed our daughter so that we might have the experience necessary to be an encourager and comfort to others, though that has happened.

Job's experience is a reminder that evil may come to all of us. Likewise, Job's response calls us to be faithful through it all—and to recognize that God honors our questions.

When we reach out to others in grief, the best thing we can do is what Job's friends initially did: to mourn with them, sit with them, and be willing to honor their pain with silence. It is not our place to offer trite explanations or to defend God: it is our place to be present, to listen, to pray, and to let grief take its course.

## Why Do We Worship God?

The heart of the accuser's challenge is the cynical proposition that Job worshiped God for selfish reasons, that his righteousness was motivated by the promise of prosperity rather than a love of obedience. One must acknowledge that a *quid pro quo* system naturally opens itself to that approach.

Think of a young attorney who takes a job in a large law firm where there are many opportunities for advancement. To achieve them, however, he or she must not only have outstanding performance reviews but also find ways to impress the partners, who are responsible for assigning promotions. While the young lawyer may want the company to do well, he or she has a deeply vested interest in doing work that will bring personal rewards as well. Likewise, if one is taught that God prospers the obedient but curses the wicked, it is in one's self-interest to pursue righteousness.

Modern believers face this same question. Why do we serve God? Some believers accept a prosperity gospel that promises wealth or success to those who have enough faith. Others believe that prayerful living will erect a "wall of protection" around them and their families. Even those who do not buy into such an approach, however, would do well to examine their motives. For many people, their primary reason for trusting Christ is to receive forgiveness and the promise of eternal life. Evangelistic training methods and pamphlets often play on this motivation, almost to the exclusion of any other: they begin by asking questions like "If you died today, are you sure that you would go to heaven?"

Sadly, it is common for people to view faith as a form of fire insurance or life insurance, a way of ensuring that they will avoid hell and land in heaven in the hereafter. Is that the point of our faith and worship? Would we be as faithful if we believed the result would be the same? Would we continue to worship God and follow the teachings of Christ if there was no connection between present behavior and future reward? Answers to questions like these give a clue as to the genuineness of our worship.

# A CREATIVE READING

If you are participating in a class, your teacher may lead the class in the following creative reading, based on the NRSV translation of Job 1:1–2:13. If not, you may find it helpful to read the story again, with characters highlighted.

## Job 1:1–2:13

**NARRATOR:** There was once a man in the land of Uz whose name was Job. That man was blameless and upright, one who feared God and turned away from evil. There were born to him seven sons and three daughters. He had seven thousand sheep, three thousand camels, five hundred yoke of oxen, five hundred donkeys, and very many servants; so that this man was the greatest of all the people of the East.

His sons used to go and hold feasts in one another's houses in turn; and they would send and invite their three sisters to eat and drink with them. And when the feast days had run their course, Job would send and sanctify them, and he would rise early in the morning and offer burnt offerings according to the number of them all; for Job said, "It may be that my children have sinned, and cursed God in their hearts." This is what Job always did.

One day the heavenly beings came to present themselves before the LORD, and Satan also came among them. The LORD said to Satan,

**LORD:** Where have you come from?

**NARRATOR:** Satan answered the LORD,

**SATAN:** From going to and fro on the earth, and from walking up and down on it.

**NARRATOR:** The Lord said to Satan,

**LORD:** Have you considered my servant Job? There is no one like him on the earth, a blameless and upright man who fears God and turns away from evil.

**NARRATOR:** Then Satan answered the LORD,

**SATAN:** Does Job fear God for nothing? Have you not put a fence around him and his house and all that he has, on every side? You have blessed the work of his hands, and his possessions have increased in the land. But stretch out your hand now, and touch all that he has, and he will curse you to your face.

**NARRATOR:** The LORD said to Satan,

**LORD:** Very well, all that he has is in your power; only do not stretch out your hand against him!

**NARRATOR:** So Satan went out from the presence of the LORD.

One day when his sons and daughters were eating and drinking wine in the eldest brother's house, a messenger came to Job and said,

**MESSENGER 1:** The oxen were plowing and the donkeys were feeding beside them, and the Sabeans fell on them and carried them off, and killed the servants with the edge of the sword; I alone have escaped to tell you.

**NARRATOR:** While he was still speaking, another came and said,

**MESSENGER 2:** The fire of God fell from heaven and burned up the sheep and the servants, and consumed them; I alone have escaped to tell you.

**NARRATOR:** While he was still speaking, another came and said,

**MESSENGER 3:** The Chaldeans formed three columns, made a raid on the camels and carried them off, and killed the servants with the edge of the sword; I alone have escaped to tell you.

**NARRATOR:** While he was still speaking, another came and said,

**MESSENGER 4:** Your sons and daughters were eating and drinking wine in their eldest brother's house, and suddenly a great wind came across the desert, struck the four corners of the house, and it fell on the young people, and they are dead; I alone have escaped to tell you.

**NARRATOR:** Then Job arose, tore his robe, shaved his head, and fell on the ground and worshiped. He said,

**JOB:** Naked I came from my mother's womb, and naked shall I return there; the LORD gave, and the LORD has taken away; blessed be the name of the LORD.

**NARRATOR:** In all this Job did not sin or charge God with wrongdoing.

One day the heavenly beings came to present themselves before the LORD, and Satan also came among them to present himself before the LORD. The LORD said to Satan,

**LORD:** Where have you come from?

**NARRATOR:** Satan answered the LORD,

**SATAN:** From going to and fro on the earth, and from walking up and down on it.

**NARRATOR:** The LORD said to Satan,

**LORD:** Have you considered my servant Job? There is no one like him on the earth, a blameless and upright man who fears God and turns away from evil. He still persists in his integrity, although you incited me against him, to destroy him for no reason.

**NARRATOR:** Then Satan answered the LORD,

**SATAN:** Skin for skin! All that people have they will give to save their lives. But stretch out your hand now and touch his bone and his flesh, and he will curse you to your face.

**NARRATOR:** The LORD said to Satan,

**LORD:** Very well, he is in your power; only spare his life.

**NARRATOR:** So Satan went out from the presence of the LORD, and inflicted loathsome sores on Job from the sole of his foot to the crown of his head. Job took a potsherd with which to scrape himself, and sat among the ashes. Then his wife said to him,

**JOB'S WIFE:** Do you still persist in your integrity? Curse God, and die.

**NARRATOR:** But he said to her,

**JOB:** You speak as any foolish woman would speak. Shall we receive the good at the hand of God, and not receive the bad?

**NARRATOR:** In all this Job did not sin with his lips.

Now when Job's three friends heard of all these troubles that had come upon him, each of them set out from his home—Eliphaz the Temanite, Bildad the Shuhite, and Zophar the Naamathite. They met together to go and console and comfort him. When they saw him from a distance, they did not recognize him, and they raised their voices and wept aloud; they tore their robes and threw dust in the air upon their heads. They sat with him on the ground seven days and seven nights, and no one spoke a word to him, for they saw that his suffering was very great.

## QUESTIONS FOR STUDY AND REFLECTION

1. What do you think it means to "fear God and turn away from evil"?

2. Have you experienced a time when you felt like Job? What was that time like for you?

3. Was it a surprise for you to learn that "the *śāṭān*" of Job 1–2 is not the same character as the "Satan" of the New Testament? Does that knowledge change your understanding of Job 1–2?

4. Do you think, as many people do, that everything—even tragedy—happens for a reason? Do you believe God actively determines everything that happens in our lives, and with a specific purpose in mind? Why or why not?

5. What events or situations in your life have caused you to ask, "Why did this happen?" or "How could God let this happen?"

## FOR INDIVIDUAL REFLECTION

Take some time and reflect on the following questions. Consider putting your thoughts into writing as a journal entry or meditation.

1. How do you feel about the idea of God making a bet with the *śāṭān* to test Job's integrity or faithfulness? Does this change or affect your image of God?

2. Do you believe God is inherently worthy of worship, or is your view of God dependent on what God has done for you lately? How would your life show your answer? Practically, if there was no clear connection between following Christ and going to heaven, would you be in church next Sunday, tithe in hand?

3. Why do you think Job's wife encouraged Job to "curse God and die"?

4. How would you define integrity? If you could keep all your material possessions, your family, and your health, but lack integrity, would those things be enough?

# NOTE

[1] For more on this subject, see Jan and Tony Cartledge, *A Whole New World* (Macon GA: Smyth & Helwys, 2005).

Session 2

# JOB'S QUESTIONING LAMENT

### Focal text: 3:1-26

The first two chapters of Job recount the story of how "the greatest man of the East" faced the severest losses imaginable while demonstrating trust beyond compare. If the story had ended there, the character of Job would have remained a superhuman icon of faith, a model of maturity to which we could hardly aspire.

But the story doesn't end there. With chapter 3, Job's inner human awakens, his patience frays, his complaints mount to the heavens, and he becomes a character with whom we can identify more readily. That is not the only change, however, for chapter 3 marks an abrupt change in literary style as well as in Job's pattern of response to tragedy. In form, the prose narrative found in the frame (Job 1–2; 42:7-17) gives way to a poetic style that characterizes the next thirty-nine chapters.

As we approach Job's sudden outburst of questions and cursing in the face of tragedy, we are confronted by important questions about divine providence and human response. Can faith be expressed in painful lamentation as well as quiet affirmation? At this point, we get little or no interpretive help, for the authoritative voice of the narrator, so present in the first two chapters, is nowhere to be found in the poetic section of the book. As Job cries out to God and argues with his friends, there is no one to offer critique or commentary on whether Job is justified in his questions, whether Job's accusers are correct in their accusations, or whether Job's reaction to their charges is appropriate. For this lengthy, poetic part of the journey, we as readers become integral participants in the dialogue. As we pore over and ponder the text, we join Job in the agonizing search for understanding.

# BIBLICAL BACKGROUND

## Speaking in Verse

As the narrator surrenders his voice, Job emerges from his seven-day silence and begins to speak for himself. When the troubled subject of God's wager opens cracked lips to speak before his three friends (3:1-2), the pliant acceptance Job had expressed in chapters 1–2 is gone. Instead, his friends—and readers—hear him speak volatile words that curse his birth (3:3-10) and question why his miserable life continues (3:11-26).

Before directly engaging Job's heartrending soliloquy, however, it would be helpful to review the characteristics of the literary style used in this section. Hebrew poetry is both like and unlike its English counterpart. With the exception of English free verse, both Hebrew and English poets speak in related phrases designed to carry a thought forward in lyrical fashion, generally following a detectable rhythm.

A primary characteristic of much (but not all) English poetry is a repetition of similar sounds that we call "rhyme." In contrast, Hebrew poetry rarely repeats sounds. Its primary distinction is a repetition of thoughts, a "rhyme" of sense rather than sound.

The basic unit of Hebrew verse is a two-line unit called a "couplet," in which the second line is roughly parallel to the first. Bible scholars generally identify three variations on the theme. The second line may repeat the sense of the first line in different words (synonymous parallelism), reinforce the first line from a contrary perspective (antithetic parallelism), or advance the thought of the first line without necessarily repeating it (synthetic or "formal" parallelism).

For example, Job 3:11 is a straightforward example of synonymous parallelism: "Why did I not die at birth, come forth from the womb and expire?" The second phrase expresses the same idea as the first, but in different words. In Job 8:20, however, the first and second lines of the verse advance the same thought in antithetical ways: "See, God will not reject a blameless person, nor take the hand of evildoers." The ideas that God will not reject the righteous and that God will not accept the wicked are opposite ways of advancing the same general thought.

A third type of parallelism, often called synthetic parallelism, is common in Job. In synthetic parallelism, the second line amplifies the thought with a related statement, as in this verse: "Yes, let that night be barren; let no joyful cry be heard in it" (3:7). In that verse, Job speaks two related, but not identical curses against the night of his conception.

Though couplets are most common, triplets also appear, as in 3:5, where Job utters a triple curse on the day of his birth, repeating the same general thought in three different ways:

> Let gloom and deep darkness claim it.
> Let clouds settle upon it;
> let the blackness of the day terrify it.

Hebrew poetry is not a slave to meter, but often follows a general pattern. English translations rarely preserve the underlying Hebrew meter, but the poetry in Job often follows a 3:3 cadence, in which each paired line contains three stressed syllables. Sometimes, for emphasis, a line will begin with an attention-grabbing word that doesn't count as part of the meter (the words translated as "See" in 8:20 and "Yes" in 3:7, both cited above, are examples).

As in English, Hebrew poetry is particularly well suited for the expression of both pain and praise, for complaint and questions, for accusations and response.

## Speaking in Curses (3:3-10)

As we come to chapter 3, the reader understands that seven days of silence have passed in which Job sat in the ashes of the family dump, scratching his festering sores, and contemplating his condition. Perhaps Job found some solace in the company of friends who sat with him and honored his silence by holding their tongues, but his grief was beyond their comprehension.

Though his tongue was still, Job's mind had been hard at work during the seven days following the last recorded words he had intoned: "Shall we receive the good at the hand of God, and not receive the bad?" (2:10). The number seven often signifies the idea of completion in biblical thought, so perhaps it is fitting that after seven days, Job has his fill of silence and the internal chaos brought on by his external suffering. Job has to find some relief, and he finds an outlet in verbal venting that voices the depth of his sorrow.

Job's wife had urged her stricken husband to curse God and die. Job, still in a state of spiritual shock, could speak no ill. Now, however, Job is ready to curse: he is still hesitant to criticize God directly, but that doesn't stop him from cursing. In his misery, Job curses the night in which he was conceived and the day he was born (3:3-10), wishing he had never seen the light of day.

You may wonder why we speak of cursing when there are no "curse words" in the text. In contemporary American culture, we tend to think of cursing (or "cussing") in terms of profane language that employs scatological or sexual words for irreverent effect. Sometimes the words are used to express displeasure or anger, but often their primary purpose is to add color or edginess to one's conversation.

In popular profanity, about the only true curse word in common usage is "damn," particularly when combined with "God," because the essence of true cursing is to wish ill upon some person. That, in fact, is what the verb "to curse" means. Modern speakers rarely think of their words as having any weight beyond their offensive effect on hearers, but many ancient peoples believed that the very speaking of the words could set in motion the wished-for events, giving an inherent power to the speaking of a curse.

In cultures that ascribe generative power to the spoken word, the uttering of a curse is a potential weapon to use against others. This was the case in the ancient Near East, where curses were commonly uttered against others. Curses could be directed toward an individual or used as a weapon of war against an entire people. For example, the familiar story of Numbers 22 recounts how the king of Moab tried to hire a shaman named Balaam to pronounce a curse on the people of Israel.

Curses could also be directed toward oneself in the case of oaths. In the biblical world, an oath consisted of a declaration or a promise to do something, combined with a self-imprecation if the statement proved false or the promise was not fulfilled. The typical form was "May God do thus and so to me if I do not . . ." (Judg 17:2; 1 Kgs 8:31).

While curses are common in Scripture, the concept of cursing God was almost unthinkable. The Bible mentions just one exception (Lev 24:10-23), and the thought of it was so distasteful that the author dared not speak directly of cursing God. Rather, in describing the case, he wrote of a young man who "blasphemed the Name in a curse" (Lev 24:11). Such blasphemy was serious business: the penalty for cursing God was death by stoning.

It was also rare for the ancients to curse a thing rather than a person. Thus, Job's cursing of the day and the night in which he was born stands out as something unusual. Job's cursing of things that are under God's control could be interpreted as a cautious means of reproaching God without cursing the deity directly.

As Job ponders his pain, he concludes, as many other disconsolate people have done, that it would be better if he had never been born. Thus, he unleashes a string of dark wishes upon the day of his birth. Note the recurring theme of deep shadows: Job calls for that day to be overwhelmed by "darkness," "gloom," "deep darkness," "clouds," and a "blackness" that terrifies (3:4-5).

Job's curses extend beyond the day of his birth to the night in which he was conceived. Retaining the theme of dark wishes, Job calls for "thick darkness," barrenness, and an absence of joy to afflict the night of his conception (3:6-7). Indeed, Job wishes "that night" would cease to exist, that it would "not rejoice among the days of the year" or "come into the number of the months." With these dark words, Job expresses a desire that the night of his conception would be blotted from the calendar, as if it had never taken place.

Why does Job appear to switch subjects by turning to the sea? Few things were more feared by the ancients than the powerful and unpredictable ocean waters. Job speaks of the night of his conception with the same abhorrence typically felt for the sea, commonly feared as the chaotic home of the primordial sea monster Leviathan. Perhaps in search of support from his friends, Job calls upon others to curse the night of his conception just as they curse the frightful sea (3:8).

The Israelites were not alone in their fear of the monstrous Leviathan. In a creation myth known among the Canaanites, Leviathan appears as a seven-headed creature that is defeated by Baal. At least one biblical text (Ps 74:12-17) also speaks of Leviathan as a multi-headed enemy that Yahweh defeats. Leviathan is also mentioned in Psalm 104:26, which says God created Leviathan as a plaything, and in Isaiah 27:1, where "Leviathan" is probably a metaphorical reference to a rival nation.

Leviathan also appears later in Job, where Yahweh speaks of the powerful beast in his second speech from the whirlwind (41:1-34). In 3:8, Job's purpose in calling on "those who are skilled to rouse up Leviathan" seems to be that the great sea dragon will rise and swallow up the lights that could bring an end to the night.

Job concludes his curse of the night with a threefold wish that its darkness would never come to an end, that the dawn would not break, that the light would not shine (3:9), "because it did not shut the doors of my mother's womb, and hid trouble from my eyes" (3:10).

Job's personification of "that night" as a conscious entity that could have prevented his conception seems to be a thinly veiled way of blaming God for his troubles. It is not the night that controls conception or governs the process of childbirth, but God (for example, see Gen 29:31 and 1 Sam 1:5). Thus, the reader wonders if Job curses the night of his conception and the day of his birth as a means of implicitly cursing the One who created both night and day—and the womb that bore him.

The prevalence of creation themes here and elsewhere in chapter 3 has led some scholars to see Job's curse as a wish that creation itself would be reversed.[1] The creation story of Genesis 1 declares that God created light apart from darkness to separate day from night, with greater lights to rule the day and lesser lights to rule the night. With these actions, God set time into motion and began the process of creation, which included the sea and all its creatures. Job, however, calls for darkness to quench the day and for night to be never-ending. He wishes that the night of his conception should cease to exist, thus violating the march of time.

In this sense, Job's curses go beyond wishing that he had never been born. If all of Job's wishes were fulfilled, they would bring the entire cosmos crashing down, returning to the dark state of pre-creation chaos. When Job cursed, he really cursed!

## Speaking in Questions (3:11-26)

When calamity strikes, our natural reaction is to ask the eternal question: "Why?" Job is no exception: he asks the question multiple times and in multiple ways. Twice Job uses a combination word that literally means "for what?" (vv. 11, 20). In v. 12, he voices a term that means "what reason?" This term is particularly interesting because we recall that Yahweh had accused the *śāṭān* of inciting him against Job "for no reason" (2:3). The reader knows, Yahweh knows, and the *śāṭān* knows that Job suffers for no reason—but poor Job does not know why his children have died, why his property has been stolen or destroyed, or why his health has failed. Surely he never imagined that his losses were the condition of a heavenly bet.

As Job emerges from his silence, he appears to move rather quickly beyond wondering why the particular tragedies took place, however. In his empty grief and ever-present pain, he moves to a deeper place of loss. He still wonders why trouble came, but frames his question to ask why a man so miserable as he should ever have seen the light of day.

### 3:11-12—Why Was I Born?

In language as plaintive as it is poetic, Job bemoans his birth through a series of pathos-filled phrases. He wonders why he did not die at birth (3:11), as a still-born child. Having failed to die *in utero* and having emerged living from the womb, Job asks why there were knees to receive him, rather than allowing him to fall to the ground and die (3:12). Having been born living and placed alive on the knees of his mother, he wonders why there were breasts to nourish a child who would grow up to wish he had never lived.

Have you ever encountered such pain that you entertained similar wishes? Job's misery is so deep that he imagines it would be better never to have known life and its attendant joys, which have been so rudely taken away.

Job would not have subscribed to Alfred, Lord Tennyson's philosophy that "It is better to have loved and lost than never to have loved at all."[2] For Job, the love and joy of his previous life did nothing to ameliorate his grief. The memory of his lost children and former health made his present state of loss even more bitter.

**"Pain Finds Its Way Everywhere"**

Pain finds its way everywhere, into my vision, my feelings, my sense of judgment; it's an infiltration.

A. Daudet, *In the Land of Pain*, ed. and trans. J. Barnes (New York: Alfred A. Knopf, 2002), 23.

Job's complaint is sometimes called a lament, and properly so, at least from an English standpoint. Job certainly laments his fate. One should note, however, that Job's words do not follow the typical literary form of biblical laments such as those found in the books of Psalms and Lamentations. Those psalms of lament typically address God directly with a complaint, but then move toward an expression of trust that God will respond with deliverance (e.g., Pss 54; 61). In contrast, Job addresses God only indirectly, if at all, and expresses no hope of deliverance beyond whatever rest the grave can afford.

### 3:13-19—Why Can't I Die?

Having wished in vain that his life had never begun, Job takes the next logical step and moves on to wish his life would end. He longs for the shadowy existence of Sheol, believing that the land of the dead would be more acceptable than the miserable, painful life he has come to know on the ash heap.

Sheol, which ancient Semites thought of as a physical place where the dead persisted in a diminished but conscious state, is described in the Old Testament as being beneath the earth (Num 16:30) or beneath the roots of the mountains (Jonah 2:6; Job 26:5-7). Most biblical references insist that it is "down," a place into which the dead "descend" (Gen 37:35; 42:38; 44:29, 31; Num 16:30, 33; Deut 32:22; Job 11:8; 21:13; Pss 55:15; 86:13; Prov 15:24; Isa 7:11; 14:11, 15; 57:9; Ezek 31:15-17; Amos 9:2).

In Sheol, it was believed, the dead existed as ghostly individuals who rested in a state of weariness and weakness (Job 3:17; Ps 88:4), with only tenuous connections to the earth or to God. Sheol was thought to be a place of dark chaos (Job 10:20-21) and grim silence (Pss 94:17; 115:17). In general, the path to Sheol was a dead-end road (Job 16:22), but popular lore believed the dead could still be consulted and caused to "come up" for the purpose of fortune-telling (1 Sam 28:13-15).

The concept of hell as a place of fiery judgment beneath the earth developed later. It owes something to the older belief in Sheol, but the two should not be confused. The New Testament word generally translated as "hell" is a Greek transliteration of the Hebrew name for the Valley of Hinnom, a deep defile near Jerusalem where garbage was dumped and fires constantly burned. Hell came to be thought of as a place of eternal punishment for the wicked only. The ancient Hebrews, however, considered Sheol to be the final destination for everyone, without regard to their earthly behavior or beliefs.

Though Job has fallen to the ash heap from his position as "the greatest man in the East," he imagines that in Sheol he will rest among his peers, with "kings and counselors of the earth" and princes rich in gold and silver (3:14-15), for Sheol does not discriminate, and none can escape its embrace.

In his staggering state of grief and loss, Job wishes that he could have bypassed life altogether and gone directly to the grave as a stillborn child (3:16). His present life is so miserable that he speaks longingly of Sheol as a near-idyllic place where the wicked no longer cause trouble, where the weary can rest, where even slaves may lounge at ease, freed from their masters (3:17-19).

### 3:20-26—Why Can I Have No Rest?

That rest, however, has been denied to Job. The itch of his sores, the pain of his disease, and the hollow emptiness of his losses leave him in turmoil. With 3:20, he returns to the "why" question, and comes as close as ever to attributing his plight to God.

Modern translations often mask Job's charge that his suffering comes at God's hands. Plaintively, he cries out, "Why is light given to one in misery, and life to the bitter in soul?" That, at least, is how it reads in the NRSV. Like the KJV and most other translations, Job's cry appears to be purely passive in its expression. Even translations like the New American Standard Version (NAS95) and the Holman Christian Standard Bible (HCSB), which often give a more literal translation, render it in a passive, indefinite way: "Why is light given?"

The Hebrew verb thus translated as "given," however, is not in the passive voice. It is the active third person form of the verb. Since no subject is stated, it should be translated "Why has he given?" or "Why has one given?" The only possible referent for the understood subject is God, for only God can give both light and life to mortals.

The NET Bible (NET) not only recognizes the active nature of the verb, but goes so far as to supply the unnamed subject, rendering 3:20 as "Why does God give light to one who is in misery, and life to those whose soul is bitter?" A footnote explains that "God" has been added for clarity.

Thus, Job draws ever closer to laying his sorrows before the divine throne and blaming his troubles directly on God. He longs for death and looks for it with the eagerness of a treasure-hunter (3:21-22), but cannot find it, for God (here he uses the divine name *Eloah*) has fenced him in.

Job's world has been turned upside down. Instead of cherishing life and looking forward to growing old, he now longs for death. The reversal of Job's fortunes is evident on every hand, as illustrated by some of the author's choices in vocabulary. In 1:8, the narrator has Yahweh refer to Job as "my servant Job," a distinguished man who is faithful and righteous in every way. In 3:19, the word "servant" again appears, but on Job's lips it is in the context of a slave who finds release from his master only in the grave.

"Servant" is not the only word that has been turned about. In 1:10, the accuser had claimed that Job served God only because God had put a "hedge" of protection around him, shielding him from trouble. In 3:23, however, Job uses the same word to complain that God has now put a hedge about him to fence him in, to confine him in a life of misery and trouble. The hedge that once protected Job has now become a prison.

As a consequence of God's actions, Job finds himself groaning through the long days and living a nightmare (3:24-25), experiencing the very things that any person would dread. A Hebrew expression in 3:35 is particularly poignant: the verse begins with a noun and verb formed from the same root. Literally, Job speaks of "the fear that I feared" or "the dread that I dreaded" having come to pass. Indeed, Job's worst nightmares have come true. For all his longing, he finds no rest, no ease, not even the grave. He has become the living personification of trouble and can no longer remain silent about it (3:26).

# THEOLOGICAL THEMES

## Curses and Questions

Is there anything right about what happened to Job? The leading citizen of Uz experienced life the way it is not supposed to be, either in the minds of theologians or in the expectations of any normal person. For a remarkably righteous man to be slapped down, to be stripped of his children, to be stricken with a cruel disease, can only raise questions of right and wrong, of justice and injustice, of what is fair and unfair. What happens to Job is neither right nor just nor fair, and to pretend otherwise is either naïve or dishonest.

But Job was an honest man. His piety had led only to pain: he knew that was not right, and he spoke the truth about it. Even so, Job's character was such that he was cautious about criticizing God directly. Surprisingly, he did not ask to have his children back, or his property, or his health. Instead, Job wished he could opt out of life altogether. Job was not the last to wish he had never been born.

Take note of the transition in Job's speech. His first response was one of acceptance in which he continued to bless God: "Naked I came from my mother's womb, and naked shall I return there; the LORD gave, and the LORD has taken away; blessed be the name of the LORD" (1:21). In his second response, voiced to his wife, Job declined to complain, even when he believed God was responsible for his trials: "Shall we receive the good at the hand of God, and not receive the bad?" (2:10). Perhaps it is significant that, while Job spoke no words of blame in this second response, neither did he speak words of blessing to God, as he did previously.

In the third phase of his response, Job moved from words of blessing and acceptance, falling silent as if the magnitude of his losses finally staggered him. When Job's silence ended, he moved into the fourth phase of response, and his words were quite different. As Job cursed his birth and cried for death, could it still be said that he "did not sin with his lips" (2:10)?

Job's curses do not mean that he has lost all faith, however. There is a sense in which his bitter words of damning life and longing to escape can be seen as an expression of hope. As Samuel Balentine has written, "To curse the forces of death and destruction may be extreme. It may be futile, even absurd. It is also an act of faith, because it refuses to believe that this is the way life is supposed to be."[3]

It is all too easy for those who are not suffering to condemn those who speak their pain, but voicing grief and asking questions suggest an inner hope for change, a hope that can become the seed of future growth in a life that is unforgettably bent, but not utterly broken.

More than one Bible story suggests that God respects our cries. Witness the weeping of David, the lamentations of Jeremiah, even the prayer of Jesus in the garden and his cry of desolation from the cross. God's response to Job's complaint will not be revealed until the end of the book, but it will eventually become clear that God had heard Job's cry, respected his complaint, and responded with care.

---

### "I Know Why the Caged Bird Sings"

I know what the caged bird feels, alas!
When the sun is bright on the upland slopes;
When the wind stirs soft through the springing grass,
And the river flows like a stream of glass;
When the first bird sings and the first bud opens,
And the faint perfume from its chalice steals—
I know what the caged bird feels!

I know why the caged bird beats his wing
Till blood is red on the cruel bars;
For he must fly back to his perch and cling
When he fain would be on the bough a-swing;
And a pain still throbs in the cold, old scars
And they pulse again with a keener sting—
I know why he beats his wing!

I know why the caged bird sings, ah me,
When his wing is bruised and his bosom sore, —
When he beats his bars and he would be free;
It is not a carol of joy or glee,
But a prayer that he sends from his heart's deep core,
But a plea, that upward to Heaven he flings—
I know why the caged bird sings!

Paul Laurence Dunbar, "Sympathy," *Black Poets of the United States, from Paul Laurence Dunbar to Langston Hughes* (Urbana: University of Illinois Press, 1973), 356.

## Providence and Pain

How do you respond to loss? It is common for people, including those who suffer tragedy, to offer glib and pat responses when calamity comes. Many people, particularly those who grew up in settings dominated by the deterministic teachings of Calvinism, are taught by parents or pastors to believe that everything happens for a reason, that even catastrophic events are somehow to be interpreted as a part of God's plan and thus to be calmly accepted.

Job's story is one in which God does figure prominently into human suffering, but that does not make his story an icon for interpreting all other suffering. Whatever point was proven via the author's portrayal of a wager between Yahweh and the *śāṭān* does not need to be repeated. Nor is there any reason to assume that every trial is a divine test of faithfulness or God's way of teaching hard lessons.

After our daughter's brutal death in 1994 made our worst nightmare come true, well-meaning people told us things like "God needed another angel in his choir" or "God only chooses the prettiest flowers for his garden." Such shallow sentiments reflect what we believe is an inadequate understanding of deity, assuming that God in heaven thinks nothing of ripping out the hearts of worshiping people in order to gain another child soprano or garden plant.

We do not believe that is the way God works. Many tragedies we face are the simple and direct result of human sin—either our sin or someone else's. God neither condones sin nor causes it. Because God grants freedom to humans, however—an essential part of what we believe it means to be created in God's image—humans may reject God's way. Whether intentionally or unintentionally, they may do hateful or harmful things that bring heartbreak and suffering to others. That is not God's desire.

One may argue that every tragedy happens within God's "permissive will" because God chose to make us free agents and permits us to do hurtful things, but there is little scriptural support for the idea that God routinely sends suffering and pain as a part of some divine plan.

This is not to suggest that we cannot learn, grow, or even find greater strength through the experience of pain. Paul taught that God works together with us to bring something good from all things (Rom 8:28). That does not mean, however, that God habitually causes suffering for the express purpose of bringing something good from it.

Job did not know what had caused the awful calamities that killed his children and evaporated his wealth. He did not forsake God. For a time, however, he believed that God had forsaken him. His bitter words of woe are those of one who believes that a life without God is worse than no life at all. Thus, even Job's audacious complaint is a declaration of faith and hope.

## LITERARY THEMES

With chapter 3, the narrative (and the narrator) of the first two chapters gives way to a poetic monologue. Poetry seems a natural outlet for highly charged emotion. Have you ever tried it? When our daughter Bethany died and our world fell in, both Jan and I sought solace—or at least an avenue for pent-up pain—in writing poetry. For me, it was often a rambling style of free verse. For Jan, it was more commonly a verse for a song.

For example, during a visit with some friends who live in New Mexico, I was feeling all dried up inside, and found the desert land an apt metaphor. In response, I wrote these words:

> The great southwestern desert,
>     so desolate and dry
>     seems hardly a place for life
> and yet on every side there are
>     tumbleweeds and scrub oaks,
>     scrappy junipers and pinyan pines.
>     Yucca plants offer their blossoms to the sky
>     while the cacti dare all to approach.
> It is a different kind of life, here in the desert—
>     a start-from-scratch
>     scratch-for-water life—
>     but it is life nonetheless.
> It is a learn-this-or-quit kind of life:
>     the world is hard,
>     but life goes on.
> I suppose that is why
>     Elijah and Elisha,
>     Jeremiah and John
>     spent time in the wilderness,

why the Spirit drove Jesus into desert lands.
There was something to learn and they needed to know:
    the world is hard,
    but life goes on.
Things that are true
    are taught time and again,
now here I stand on sunbaked sand—
    the lesson is hard,
    but life goes on.

One need not look far in books of poetry to find verse that grows from roots of pain. Even dark and dismal musings can be a prelude to new hope and new birth.

## SPIRITUALITY AND MINISTRY THEMES

As discussed above, pain and sorrow can become doorways into a new way of thinking, one that is less innocent but wiser. It is an experience that goes beyond the optimistic proverb that "every cloud has a silver lining" (or the canine version: "for every trip to the vet, there's a car ride").

Thoughtfully, prayerfully working through periods of pain can lead to a life with less surface color but added richness beneath, like tropical waters where the bright aqua and teal of the shallows gives way to cerulean and deeper blue as the depth increases.

Such inner growth is neither easy nor automatic. It requires effort. It must be intentional. It often begins with asking "Why?" but must be willing to move on when no satisfactory answer is forthcoming.

In Luke 13:1-5, Jesus had the best opportunity we know of to explain why bad things happen to good people. A curious crowd asked him about a case of domestic terrorism in which Roman soldiers had massacred a group of Galilean men as they worshiped at the temple. They wanted to know why such a thing should happen, or why God would allow it. Jesus himself brought up another case in which a tower collapsed and people died for no apparent reason. The April 2007 massacre of thirty-two students and teachers at Virginia Tech, the almost routine murder of civilians in Iraq, and the ongoing genocide in Darfur remind us that such things still happen.

When people crowded around Jesus in hopes of an explanation, he offered no "why." Indeed, Jesus suggested that "Why?" is the wrong question. The important question is "What next?" Those of whom Jesus spoke apparently died without entering a relationship with Christ. Physical death is inevitable, but eternal death is not. Jesus stated that those who died were no worse sinners than other people in Galilee or Jerusalem: they did not die because they were bad people. The lesson to be learned, Jesus said, was "unless you repent, you will all perish just as they did" (Luke 13:5). Repentance would not prevent physical death, but could open a doorway to eternal life. "What next?" was more important than "Why?"

Job's complaint, though dark, also has the potential to become a doorway. Recognizing wrong, even complaining about it, can be a step toward the hope of something better. Job's lament offers little evidence of such hope, but the fact that he keeps on listening, thinking, crying, and complaining through many chapters yet to come suggests that he has not surrendered to hopelessness, but continues to yearn for something better.

The recognition of wrong and the yearning for God to make things right may give rise to the hope of better days, as one sees more explicitly in Lamentations 3:19-24. Hope, ultimately, is the root of faith. Paul spoke to the Colossians of "the faith and love that spring from the hope that is stored up for you in heaven" (Col 1:5, NIV). Job cursed his birth and the light that had been given to him, but even his dark wishes contained seeds of hope for a brighter day.

## STUDY QUESTIONS

1. If you had been present and heard Job's lament, what would you have said to Job?

2. Have there ever been outward circumstances or inner failures that have led you to feel as Job felt? Have you experienced situations that have made you long for death?

3. The concept of bitter lament as an expression of hope may not seem self-evident. Can you think of other ways to describe how complaints and curses may yet be evidence of hope?

4. We all experience pain, though not to the same degree. Some are better stewards of their pain than others. What do you think it means to be a good steward of one's pain?

## QUESTIONS FOR PERSONAL REFLECTION

Take some time to reflect on the following questions. Consider putting your thoughts into writing as a journal entry or meditation.

1. Have you ever found solace or an emotional outlet through reading or writing poetry? Try it the next time you face a time of difficulty.

2. Can you tell God that you are angry or disappointed when things don't turn out as you think they should? Is it okay to complain to God or be angry with God? Can you name a situation or time when you did so?

# NOTES

[1] Samuel Balentine, *Job*, Smyth & Helwys Bible Commentary (Macon GA: Smyth & Helwys, 2006), 84.

[2] "In Memoriam A. H. H.," *Tennyson's Poetry*, selected and edited by R. W. Hill, Jr. (New York/London: W.W. Norton and Co., 1971), XXVII, 13-16. Also available at http://charon.sfsu.edu/tennyson/inmemoriam.html. The context, from stanza 4, is:

I hold it true, whate'er befall;

I feel it, when I sorrow most;

'Tis better to have loved and lost

Than never to have loved at all.

[3] Balentine, *Job*, 97.

# JOB'S ACCUSING FRIENDS

### Focal text: 4:1–14:22

Humans love to talk. Most of the time, our conversations consist of shallow pleasantries or innocuous information sharing. At other times, our conversations get personal, and when they get personal, they sometimes become hurtful. Have you ever been involved in an exchange of words that included accusing or hurtful comments, and the longer the discourse lasted, the more prickly and uncomfortable it became? Job could identity with that scenario. One might think the misery Job expressed in his woeful lamentations of chapter 3 could grow no worse. One might hope the presence of his friends might bring comfort. Sadly, Job's torment only increased when three friends who had been sitting and listening to him began to speak.

In this session we will examine excerpts from a lengthy dialogue between Job and three friends that takes place in chapters 4–14. While that large a text seems ambitious, keep in mind that these selections are from the first of three rounds of dialogue between Job and his "comforters."

## BIBLICAL BACKGROUND

The larger context of conversation between Job and his friends covers no less than thirty-three chapters, beginning with chapter 4 and continuing through chapter 37. The author has constructed the exchanges between Job and his three visitors (ch. 4–27) in such a way that there are three cycles of dialogues (you may want to refer back to the outline in ch. 1, "Job's Innocent Affliction"). In each cycle, with minor exceptions, Job's companions take turns making speeches to him. The three always speak in the order Eliphaz-Bildad-Zophar, with the exception of the final round, in which Zophar does not speak. Each friend's speech is followed by a pained response from Job.

The long back-and-forth between Job and his three friends is followed by a hymn in praise of God's wisdom (ch. 28) that is not assigned to any speaker. Job offers what appears to be a closing argument in chapters 29–31, but then a fourth speaker bullies his way into the conversation. A brash visitor named Elihu, who claims to be younger but wiser than the rest, speaks nonstop in chapters 32–37. Elihu speaks as if he has silently listened to the preceding conversations, and he claims to clarify and correct any shortcomings in the previous arguments. Notably, Job does not respond to Elihu, as he does to the other speakers. Neither does God. Yahweh will have a word for Eliphaz, Bildad, and Zophar (42:7-9), but does not acknowledge Elihu at any point. This and other evidence suggests that chapters 32–37 were composed and inserted by a later writer who thought some of the previous statements deficient and sought to correct them.

In our survey of representative excerpts from the first cycle of conversations between Job and his three friends, we discover that the friends are more interested in accusing Job than in understanding him. This is surprising, because 2:11-13 suggests that Job's friends had shown true compassion when they first came to "console and comfort him." At their initial meeting, the friends "raised their voices and wept aloud" in an apparent heartfelt response to Job's plight. Like the friend of a cancer victim who shaves his head to show solidarity with his friend's hair loss after chemotherapy, the friends tore their robes, threw dust over their heads, and joined Job in the dust. They sat with Job in silent vigil for seven days and nights, "for they saw that his suffering was very great" (2:12-13).

Thus, the friends initially honor Job's unspeakable grief by their unspeaking presence. One begins to wonder, however, if they are just patiently waiting for Job to confess his sin. After Job's unanticipated outburst of cursing and questioning, their sympathies turn from Job to God, for they assume Job is being punished for some reason yet unknown to them. When Job expresses displeasure with God's behavior, his friends quickly jump to God's defense, insisting that Job must have done something to deserve discipline. Stubbornly, Job remains equally insistent that he is innocent and undeserving of his fate.

In their speeches, Job's friends build on the same theme and follow a predictable pattern. Each of the friends' speeches begins with an introductory section that poses a rhetorical question about the ways of God (4:2-6; 8:2-7; 11:2-6), followed by a series of comments and cautions (4:7–5:7; 8:8-19; 11:7-12). Each speech concludes with a reminder that Job could be restored if he would only heed the speaker's advice to acknowledge his sin and repent (5:17-27; 8:20-22; 11:13-20).

Job listens to his friends but flatly rejects their calm insistence that God cannot be questioned. Job maintains his innocence (6:28-30; 9:21; 10:7) and implies that God's inconsistent behavior toward him calls into question their entire understanding of how God relates to humans. He dares to suggest that someone should confront God with the question "What are you doing?" (9:12).

**Trust and Obey**

The words of the hymn "Trust and Obey" provide but one example of a common theology that nurtures faith in the inscrutable providence of God. Verse 2, which speaks of the burden of suffering, exemplifies (from a Christian perspective) the encouragement such theology offers to persons like Job:

> Not a burden we bear, Not a sorrow we share
> But our toil He doth richly repay; Not a grief or a loss,
> Not a frown or a cross, But is blest if we trust and obey.

## Eliphaz (chs. 4–5, focal text—4:1-11; 5:8, 17-27)

Eliphaz always speaks first, and appears to be the elder and leader of the three. Near the end of the book, in 42:7, the narrator says God spoke directly to Eliphaz to express divine displeasure with him and his two friends, further indicating that he was the acknowledged leader.

Eliphaz's first address is a curious mixture of humility and condescension. On the one hand, he speaks as if afraid that Job might take offense (4:2). On the other hand, he insists that Job is now in need of advice (4:3-4). Although Job is commonly remembered as a model of patience and piety, Eliphaz charges that Job has become impatient (4:5) and has lost touch with his characteristic integrity (4:6).

As usual, Eliphaz lays down a charge that the other friends will build upon. Using the language of traditional wisdom but speaking as if from personal experience, Eliphaz sets out the premise that God blesses the righteous but punishes the wicked (4:7-9). One reaps what one sows, he says, voicing a common truism that appears elsewhere in Scripture (Prov 22:8; Hos 8:7; 10:13; Eccl 7:3; Gal 6:7-8). Because he believes that Job has sinned, Eliphaz is not surprised that Job has felt the blast of God's anger (4:10-11).

In his speech, Eliphaz goes on to reinforce his position by asserting that a frightening spirit had came to him in a dream and asked, "Can mortals be righteous before God? Can human beings be pure before their Maker?" (4:17).

This appears to be a direct contradiction to Job's claim of innocence, confirmed by a vision.

Not content to stop there, Eliphaz goes on in 5:1-7 to press the thorn of his criticism even deeper by placing Job in the company of fools who suffer but don't understand that "human beings are born to trouble, just as sparks fly upward" (5:7).

Piously, Eliphaz tells Job to seek God, as he has done: "As for me, I would seek God, and to God I would commit my cause . . ." (5:8). Eliphaz then praises God as one who created the earth, who rules over its inhabitants, and who administers punishment to the wicked (5:9-16).

Perhaps Eliphaz is playing off of Job's earlier wish for darkness and blackness to come over the day of his birth (3:5) when he implies that Job's darkness is his own doing. Those who are "wise in their own craftiness" will "meet with darkness in the daytime, and grope at noonday as in the night" (5:13-14), he says.

Eliphaz closes his speech (5:17-27) by listing specific blessings that are bound to come Job's way—if Job will accept his plight as well-deserved divine discipline: "How happy is the one whom God reproves; therefore do not despise the discipline of the Almighty" (5:17).

Samuel Balentine comments that Eliphaz's self-satisfied certainty makes him "more like a dogmatic theologian than a pastoral counselor."[1] That position is reinforced by his condescending conclusion: "See, we have searched this out; it is true. Hear, and know it for yourself" (5:27).

Eliphaz was a man who has his mind made up and wouldn't tolerate questions that might threaten his theology. Unfortunately, such a stance prevented him from being willing to hear Job's response with an open mind.

## Job's Response to Eliphaz (chs. 6–7, focal text—6:1-13, 24-30; 7:16-21)

While Eliphaz is convinced of Job's guilt, Job is equally certain of his innocence. As we learned from the first verse of the book, Job "was blameless and upright, one who feared God and turned away from evil." He has never ceased to seek God, despite Eliphaz's advice that he needs to begin.

We learn from Job's response that he has listened carefully to Eliphaz, but he refuses to accept his friend's glib recitation of traditional wisdom. Job knows firsthand the burden of his calamities: if piled on one side of a balance scale, he says, they would outweigh all the sands of the sea (6:2-3).

Job recognizes God as the source of his sorrow. He has hinted at it previously (3:23), but now he speaks outright:

> For the arrows of the Almighty are in me;
> my spirit drinks their poison;
> the terrors of God are arrayed against me. (4:4)

The Bible often speaks of God as an archer (Deut 32:23-24; Ezek 5:16; Lam 3:12-13; Pss 7:13; 38:2; 64:7), but this is the only time God is charged with using poisoned arrows.

Eliphaz had spoken of God as one who "wounds" and "strikes" as a means of discipline, but who also "binds up" and "heals" (5:18). Job does not see God as a well-meaning disciplinarian, however. In his mind, God has become like an enemy warrior whose sharp weapons and fierce "terrors" have made him long for death.

Eliphaz had portrayed God as a healer to the faithful, but Job sees God as his tormentor. His only hope is that God would finish the job by "crushing" him and "cutting him off" (6:8-9). That would be some "consolation," Job says: he would willingly go to his death in the knowledge that he has "not denied the words of the Holy One" (6:10).

Job declares that he does not have the strength of stones or of bronze that would allow him to stand against his trials; he is exhausted and worn, he has nothing left (6:11-13).

As he suffers in the face of his friends' accusations, Job grows bold and accuses them of being fair-weather friends. Friends have a right to expect loyalty, but Job senses that his friends have turned against him in his trouble. They are like a streambed that has gone dry (6:15-17), like a mirage that confounds desert travelers (6:18-20). Job says he would gladly learn from honest words that teach him something he doesn't know, but that is not what he hears from Eliphaz. Instead, Job says, Eliphaz seems afraid to face the depths of Job's calamity (6:21). Eliphaz has not sought to understand him and has listened to his words as if they were nothing more than whistling wind (6:24-26).

Have you ever had a friend to doubt you, even when you were telling the truth? Job knew that feeling. He challenged his friends to take a hard look at him and see the truth in his words (6:28-30). He wanted them to believe him and to believe in him—not to accuse him of wrongdoing. Job wanted someone to help him understand why his world had been turned upside down, not just accuse him of pulling the lever of wickedness.

Job had always believed the same theology shared by his friends, but his innocent suffering had called those beliefs into question. Job wanted to understand why God turned against him in spite of his faithfulness, but his friends were too afraid or too self-certain to enter Job's world of pain and explore the question.

Job wanted to know why God would attack a righteous man. Job's friends wanted to know why a formerly faithful but presumably sinful man would refuse to come clean.

**"Grief"**

Eyes
That are frozen
From not crying.

Heart
That knows
No way of dying.

L. Hughes, "Grief," *The Collected Poems of Langston Hughes,*
ed. A. Rampersad (New York: Vantage Books, 1994), 334.

As Job continues to speak in chapter 7, he recounts the depth of his pain and the magnitude of his sorrows (7:1-6). With 7:7, however, Job shifts his address from his friends to God. In a forlorn prayer, Job unleashes the inner misery that makes him long for death (7:7-10). With nothing left to lose, Job no longer fears to speak his mind and give vent to the anguish of his soul (7:11).

Job questions God directly. He wonders how he has become a threat, like the sea or a dragon, that deserves such severe sanction that he is left longing for death (7:12-15) and loathing his life (7:16).

With 7:17, Job puts a sarcastic twist on the psalmist's wondering words of Psalm 8:4. For the psalmist, the words "What are human beings that you are mindful of them, mortals that you care for them?" reflect humble awe, but in Job's mouth, "What are human beings, that you make so much of them, that you set your mind on them?" becomes a pitiable complaint.

While the psalmist gloried in God's care for humankind, Job wished only that God would leave him alone and stop causing him pain (7:18-20). Job admitted to no transgression, but even if he had sinned, Job wondered why God should not be willing to forgive and cease his tormenting visitations (7:21). Job was convinced that any such pardon would come too late for a man already dead and buried in the earth, however. Even if God were to seek him out, Job says, "I shall not be."

## Bildad (ch. 8, focal text—8:1-7, 20-22)

Did you ever have a teacher or other authority figure speak to you with condescension, as if looking down their nose? Bildad's speech has that kind of effect. Like Eliphaz, Bildad makes no attempt to enter Job's world of pain and confusion. He responds to Job's passionate questions with the cold demeanor of a pompous professor who instructs a forgetful student.

Bildad begins by picking up on Job's complaint that Eliphaz had treated his words as wind (6:26). He disdainfully describes Job's words as "a great wind," as blustery words spoken in error (8:2).

Bildad asks the question, "Does God pervert justice?" (8:3). That, of course, is precisely what Job has charged. Knowing his own innocence, he believes that God has broken the rules and attacked the righteous. But Bildad insists that Job is wrong: if his children died, it was because they had sinned (8:4). If Job will but repent of his own sin and become truly "pure and upright," God will certainly restore him (8:5-7).

With a series of illustrations drawn from nature (8:8-19), Bildad builds toward the unmistakable charge that Job must be guilty. As the papyrus plant will die without water, those who depart from God will perish, he says; as a spider trusts in a "house" that is easily crushed, the wicked misplace their confidence. "God will not reject a blameless person, nor take the hand of evildoers" (8:20), he concludes.

Bildad's mind is filled with certainty that the problem is not with God's justice, but with Job's denial of it. Job needs only to trust in God to do what is right, for "He will yet fill your mouth with laughter, and your lips with shouts of joy" (8:21).

## Job's Response to Bildad (chs. 9–10, focal text—9:1-24; 10:1-22)

As Job listens to Bildad's arrogant words and simplistic answers, he appears to lose patience with his consoler. Job is plagued by questions more painful than the boils on his skin, but Bildad refuses to take them seriously. Instead, he reflects the traditional "if . . . then" theology of the Deuteronomist, a clear-cut compact in which righteousness earns rewards and sin begets sorrow.

Having suffered despite his innocence, Job loses faith in that theology. He now fantasizes about challenging God in court (9:3), but knows that arguing with God is fruitless. He guesses that God is so far beyond human comprehension, so powerful beyond human might, that all he can hope for is mercy (9:4-15).

Indeed, Job concludes that, even if he had the power to summon God, he would find no divine concern for his complaints (9:16). In Job's recent experience, God has brought him only storms and bitterness (9:17-18); the Lord's overwhelming strength would make any attempt at questioning or complaining fruitless (9:19).

During the "war on terror," we have often heard of torturous interrogations that lead prisoners to say things that may or may not be true. Job knows he is blameless, but he fears that the terrifying presence of God will wring confessions from him despite his innocence (9:20-21). Even so, Job cannot hold back his complaint that might does not make right, that God has inexplicably violated timeless promises, that "he destroys both the blameless and the wicked" (9:22).

The depth of Job's sorrow grows in part from his faith that God does in fact control what goes on in the world. Creation, however, is no longer beautiful to Job, who sees a world that has been given over to wickedness and blind judges (9:23). Job can only conclude that God is responsible: "if it is not he, who then is it?" (9:24).

Job seems to consider other possibilities in 9:25-35, but returns to his core complaint in chapter 10. Emboldened by sorrow, with nothing to lose, Job speaks brashly and boldly. He vents his bitterness and challenges God to explain why wickedness should triumph while the innocent suffer loss (10:1-3). What Job understands is that he believes God does *not* understand what it is like to see the issue from a mortal's perspective (10:5-6) and feel betrayed by God (10:7).

Job asks a series of questions laced with metaphors related to creation. He wonders why the God who formed him like clay (10:8-9), who curdled him into being like cheese (10:10), who clothed him with skin, who knit him together with sinews (10:11), and who once loved him with steadfast love (10:12), would harbor a hidden purpose to harm him (10:13-14). Job could understand God's heavy hand if he had indeed sinned, but he cannot comprehend why God would hunt down an innocent man and continue sending fresh troops against him (10:15-17).

With 10:18-22, Job seems spent, and returns to the same sad longing for nonexistence he first expressed in chapter 3. Now, however, Job's questions are not impersonal wonderings like "Why did I not die at birth?" (3:11). Now, Job's queries are pointed and addressed directly to God: "Why did you bring me forth from the womb?" (10:18-19). Job wishes his heavenly antagonist would leave him alone and let him die in peace. He longs to enter "the land of gloom and deep darkness" where even "light is like darkness" (10:20-22). Job's language, reminiscent of 3:5-6, reflects a darkness of soul that leads him to long for the darkness of death. Perhaps, echoing his wife's sentiments in 2:9, he hopes his direct challenge to the deity will hasten death's arrival.

## Zophar (ch. 11, focus text—11:1-6, 13-20)

Job is not the only participant in the conversation who is losing patience. Zophar, the third friend, seems to be fed up with Job's stubbornness. He wishes that God would speak up and answer Job's "multitude of words" that "babble" and "mock" God (11:1-3), words that claim innocence when guilt seems so apparent to everyone but Job (11:4).

"Oh, that God would speak, and open his lips to you, and that he would tell you the secrets of wisdom!" (11:5-6a), he says. Zophar, however, has no real expectation that God might thunder a message from the sky, so he confidently intones a message in God's behalf, as one who fully understands the secrets of wisdom.

Zophar's accusations drive the nails even deeper than the charges leveled by Eliphaz and Bildad. "Know then," he says, "that God exacts of you less than your guilt deserves" (11:6b). Zophar seems to believe not only that Job is guilty of some hidden sin, but that his constant claims to innocence are compounding his guilt.

One can hardly expect to understand the fullness of God, Zophar says, for it is higher than heaven, deeper than Sheol, longer than the earth, and wider than the seas (11:7-9). Such a God, Zophar says, makes no errors in judgment and no mistakes in recognizing iniquity (11:10-11).

Daring to stretch the lines of their previous friendship, Zophar implies that Job is acting foolishly, like a hollow-headed man. With disparaging words, he concludes that Job has become such a hopeless case that he is no more likely to get understanding than a wild ass is likely to give birth to a human (11:12).

Like his companions, however, Zophar insists there is hope for Job if only he will turn his heart toward God (11:13) and forsake his sin (11:14). If he would only repent, Zophar promises, Job could rest in security and put misery behind him (11:15-17). Zophar says, "And you will have confidence, because there is hope; you will be protected and take your rest in safety. You will lie down, and no one will make you afraid; many will entreat your favor" (11:18-19).

Zophar's assurance is double-edged, however. The flip side is that those who remain in wickedness will lose all possibility of escape, and their only hope "is to breathe their last" (11:20)—precisely the hope Job had earlier expressed.

## Job's Response to Zophar (chs. 12–14, focal text—12:1-6; 13:1-5; 14:7-17)

Job responds to Zophar with his lengthiest speech to this point, second in length only to his closing arguments in chapters 29–31. The speech addresses Job's friends initially (12:1–13:3), but gradually morphs (13:4-19) into a prayer directed toward God (13:20–14:22).

Job's first response to Zophar's speech seems to address all three friends, not Zophar alone. All of them have spoken to him with condescension, as if he is a child to be taught and needs only their wise counsel to turn around the shambles his life has become.

Job cannot resist a sarcastic comment: "No doubt you are the people, and wisdom will die with you" (12:2). Then he insists, "But I have understanding as well as you. I am not inferior to you. Who does not know such things as these?" (12:3).

In his grief, Job protests that his friends treat him as a laughingstock and refuse to believe in him. They rely too easily on facile assumptions and fail to understand Job's misery (12:4-5). Job is the only one willing to struggle with the existential question of why the innocent suffer while the wicked—even idolaters—live securely, and it is a lonely struggle (12:6).

Job challenges his friends to learn from nature (12:7-8), a common appeal in Wisdom literature. In 12:9, surprisingly, he speaks in words almost identical to those in Isaiah 41:20b: "Who among all these does not know that the hand of the LORD has done this?" Job continues to maintain his innocence. He holds to faint hope and expresses painful praise (12:14-25), but remains at a loss to explain what has happened to him.

Of one thing Job is certain: his friends are no help. He knows as much as they do (13:2). They whitewash Job's dark pain with lies like worthless     physicians who cannot heal, and would be more helpful if they would only be silent and listen to him (13:4-6).

**Lodged**

The rain to the wind said,
    "You push and I'll pelt."
They so smote the garden bed
That the flowers actually knelt,
And lay lodged—though not dead.
I know how the flowers felt.

Robert Frost, "Lodged," *The Poetry of Robert Frost*, ed. E. C. Lathem (New York: Henry Holt and Company, 1969), 250.

With no help from his friends, Job again longs to bring his case before God (13:3), something his small-minded friends would never dare to do (13:7-12). Job seems on the verge of doing what his wife advised in 2:9—he does not plan to "curse God and die," but he does intend to question God, even if he dies (13:13-15). One way or the other, Job will have his say.

In the final part of his speech, Job turns to prayer and pleads that God would reverse course, reveal what instigated the attacks, stop hiding, and remember that Job is only mortal (13:20–14:6).

With 14:7-17, Job moves on to ponder questions of life, death, and the possibility of life beyond death. He has seen how trees, though laid low, may grow back from their roots (14:7-9). He has also seen that mortals are more like a lake that dries up: they "lie down and do not rise up again" (14:10-12). Job's last hope seems to be that God might hide him in Sheol until the divine wrath passes, and then "remember" him at a later time (14:13).

Job has little optimism, however. Painfully, sorrowfully, he asks, "If mortals die, will they live again?" (14:14). Job knows nothing of the heavenly hope that would later bring comfort to followers of Christ, but he yearns for a new life beyond the near death he is experiencing. He longs for God to favor him as in former days (14:15), beckoning him to a new life in which his transgressions are covered and his sins are not counted (14:16-17).

Job aches for this, but he does not believe it will happen. As mountains crumble with the passage of time, so humans are worn away before God's power, he thinks. They do not give their years to praise, but "feel only the pain of their own bodies, and mourn only for themselves" (14:22).

With these words, Job paints a self-portrait of his sorrow. His hope hangs by the thinnest thread, and his friends are no help at all.

## THEOLOGICAL THEMES

Could you give a short summary of your own theology if someone asked? Job's friends would certainly have no problem in responding. Their beliefs clearly reflect the "if . . . then" theology that finds its clearest expression in passages like Deuteronomy 28, and underlies most of the Old Testament. Job is equally familiar with that theology, which promises divine blessings for human obedience, and has followed it all of his life. That is why he is in such a quandary: Job's comfortable worldview has been turned upside down and his previous understanding of reality no longer applies. Job knows that he has lived up to the "if . . ." part of the traditional approach to God, but he suddenly gets a very different ". . . then" than expected.

When we sit in the dust and listen to Job pour out his heart, we are led to join Job in questioning the traditional understanding of how one relates to God. Are blessings guaranteed for the righteous? Should earthly troubles necessarily be regarded as signs of heavenly displeasure? The foundational beliefs upon which Job had built his life seemed no longer to be set in stone, but were crumbling into sand.

Should this lead us to reject the traditional view of the divine-human relationship as inaccurate or inadequate? Is there more to be said about the ways of God in the lives of mortals? Dealing with Job's dilemma demands that we pose the question.

The text could also lead us to ponder another question with even more personal implications. What if Job should decide to surrender to his friends' advice and repent of sin, even if he didn't believe he had committed it—but did so only in hopes of having blessings restored? Would Job then be guilty of precisely what the *śāṭān* had charged in 1:9, bowing down to God for selfish reasons only?

As contemporary Christians, do we serve God only for what we get—or hope to get—out of the relationship? Do we profess faith and seek baptism primarily because we want to avoid hell and gain heaven? Do we worship and tithe and serve in part because we hope to gain God's favor and be rewarded with prosperity or protection?

Does our prayer life focus mainly on requests for physical health, successful relationships, or material blessings? And let's consider the bottom-line question: ultimately, if serving God included no promise of eternal life and no assurance of any connection between spiritual devotion and personal prosperity, would we still serve God?

## LITERARY THEMES

Do you like poetry? Have you ever heard anyone outside of a Shakespearean play converse by speaking extemporaneous verse? That rarely happens, and the image of Job and his friends carrying on extensive dialogues in poetry seems a bit far-fetched. One must suspect, then, that the writer has given poetic shape to the putative conversations for a particular purpose.

Job, like Proverbs and Ecclesiastes, is part of the Bible's Wisdom literature. Such writings were commonly set forth in the form of poetry: as such, the writing seems more thought-through and thought-provoking, heavy with meaning but open to analysis.

In some ways, such poetic conversation is not unlike contemporary hip-hop or rap music that is more spoken than sung. Hip-hop lyrics lean heavily on rhyme and wordplay, making them catchy and memorable. Many young people listen to the songs over and over, memorizing the words, debating their meaning, carrying the original singer's message or feelings forward.

It's not necessary to read Job with underlying tracks of bass and percussion, but it helps to remember that the words were couched in poetic form, in part to make them memorable.

## SPIRITUALITY AND MINISTRY THEMES

Can pain lead to a deeper connection with God? Job's questions and complaints remind the reader that spirituality and faith have roots in sorrow as well as joy: God may be encountered in deep, rugged valleys as well as upon high, scenic mountaintops. Even Job's pained plea for God to leave him alone (7:16) is in truth an act of reaching for God.

In his commentary on Job, Samuel Balentine expressed this thought beautifully: "When pushed to the limits, perhaps this is the ultimate expression of faith: to pray without the certainty of a hearing, to believe when experience does not warrant it, to carve out life, step by painful step, even when death seems more desirable."[2]

The encounter between Job and his friends speaks pointedly to those times when we minister to suffering people. Job's friends refused to enter the world of his pain or to entertain the questions he raised. They dared not risk their own sense of safety and security by joining Job's questioning efforts to dig for understanding. As a result, they defended God and put Job on the defensive.

Is their response so different from that of contemporary believers who "comfort" grieving people with popular platitudes like "God knows what he is doing," "everything happens for a reason," or "one day you'll understand"?

Some people might find comfort in these words, but those who know something of Job's pain and loss will not. Should we believe that God intentionally causes the death or disease or disaster that has brought suffering to our lives? Is there any motivation to worship a God who kills children, who causes cancer, who aims hurricanes at one city but not another— even in response to prayer? Those who suffer long to hear of a God who joins them in their suffering rather than causing their pain.

The negative example of Job's friends suggests that true ministry to the hurting comes when we are willing to give up any effort to defend God, and instead take the risk of entering the pain of those who suffer. Those who grieve will find their greatest comfort in those who are willing to sit in their world, respect their questions, and, by their steady presence, offer the promise of hope.

## "Speak What We Feel"

In the final scene of *King Lear,* the king comes center stage holding his dead daughter Cordelia in his arms. By play's end, the once proud and sovereign monarch is broken and despondent. Through his own foolishness his kingdom lies in ruin; through his own scheming, his family is shattered. Holding the limp body of his beloved daughter, Lear moans:

Why should a dog, a horse, a rat have life,
And thou no breath at all? Thou shalt come
    no more,
Never, never, never, never, never!

With these words, the king collapses and dies. Witnessing this grief-filled moment, the Duke of Albany offers a final summation:

The weight of this sad time we must obey;
Speak what we feel, not what we ought to
    say.

(King Lear, Act V, sc. 3, lines 305-307, 322-23)

# STUDY QUESTIONS

1. Do contemporary Christians serve God only for what we get—or hope to get—out of the relationship? Do we profess faith and seek baptism primarily because we want to avoid hell and gain heaven? Do we worship and tithe and serve in hope of gaining God's favor? Do we pray primarily for protection and blessing?

2. The words of Eliphaz, Bildad, and Zophar imply that neither God nor orthodox beliefs about God can be questioned. What do you think? Have you ever questioned God's purposes—or whether God even has a purpose in everything that happens?

3. How does Job's experience speak to our efforts to provide comfort to the hurting, understanding to the confused, or hope to the despairing? Are we more likely to defend God for fear that our own convictions might collapse, or are we willing to risk entering the world of their experience, allowing them to voice questions (even curses!) without judgment?

4. Is your understanding of God something akin to the "if . . . then" contractual relationship expressed with such certainty by Job's friends? If that is the case, is your relationship with God truly one of faith, or could it better be described as a rational investment that expects a guaranteed return?

5. What is the role of human faith in the face of divine silence?

## QUESTIONS FOR PERSONAL REFLECTION

1. If you had no promise of eternal life and no assurance of a connection between spiritual devotion and personal prosperity, would you still serve God? Why or why not?

2. Have you ever gone through a time when the foundational beliefs upon which you had built your life no longer seemed to work? How did that time affect your faith and practice?

## NOTES

[1] Samuel Balentine, *Job*, Smyth & Helwys Bible Commentary (Macon GA: Smyth & Helwys, 2006), 104.

[2] Ibid., 145.

Session 4

# JOB'S CONFRONTATIONAL GOD

### Focal text: 38:1–42:17

Have you ever wanted to call God into court? I suspect that most of us have a list of questions we'd like to ask God if we ever get the chance. The question at the top of our list probably has to do with why we or why someone we know had to suffer.

Every person who lives long enough will face trials and troubles. Some of our wounds will be self-inflicted, but others may come with no warning and for no apparent reason. They may leave us wanting to call God into court, to question Yahweh face to face, to ask "What were you doing?"

That is precisely what Job did. He pleaded for a personal conversation with God because he believed God had some explaining to do. Beginning with chapter 38, Job got his wish, and it was more than he had bargained for.

## BIBLICAL BACKGROUND

Job often spoke of his longing for an audience with God, and nowhere more clearly than in chapter 23 in his third response to Eliphaz. "Oh, that I knew where I might find him," Job cries, "that I might come even to his dwelling!" (23:3). Job imagines what it would be like to "lay my case before him" (23:4) and "understand what he would say to me" (23:5). Job seems confident that God would not overwhelm him with "the greatness of his power" but "would give heed to me" (23:6).

Despite this show of confidence, Job also complains that he cannot find God, no matter which direction he turns (23:8-9). The more he talks, the less confident Job grows. He is certain that God observes his every move and knows

### "Scared I'd Hafta Face Up to What I Didn't Do"

Part of Harper Lee's Pulitzer Prize-winning novel, *To Kill a Mockingbird*, is the story of a black man, Tom Robinson, who has been falsely accused of raping Mayella Ewell, a white woman. When he is brought to trial, Robinson must answer the questions of Mr. Gilmer, the prosecutor. The following courtroom exchange is pertinent for reflecting on Elihu's attack on Job's claim to be innocent:

(Mr. Gilmer): "Didn't Mr. Ewell run you off the place, boy?"
(Robinson): "No suh, I don't think he did."
"Don't think, what do you mean?"
"I mean I didn't stay long enough for him to run me off."
"You're very candid about this, why did you run so fast?"
"I says I was scared, suh."
"If you had a clear conscience, why were you scared?"
"Like I says before, it weren't safe for any nigger to be in a—fix like that."
"But you weren't in a fix—you testified that you were resisting Miss Ewell. Were you so scared that she'd hurt you, you ran, a big buck like you?"
"No suh, I's scared I'd be in court, just like I am now."
"Scared of arrest, scared you'd have to face up to what you did?"
"No suh, scared I'd hafta face up to what I didn't do."

H. Lee, *To Kill a Mockingbird* (New York: Popular Library Edition, 1960), 200-201.

---

that he has held to his integrity (23:10-12), but Job no longer sees a direct connection between human behavior and divine response.

In Job's closing arguments of chapters 29–31, his final words before the text is sidetracked by a lengthy interruption from Elihu (chs. 32–37), he boldly shouts "Let the Almighty answer me!" (31:15). In chapter 38, Job gets an Almighty response.

When God appears to Job, it is in the form of an awe-inspiring whirlwind. That should not surprise us, because storms commonly accompany theophanies (appearances of God) in Old Testament writings (Ezek 1:4; Nah 1:3; Zech 9:14).

When Yahweh first speaks from the whirlwind, the words seem as blustery and impatient as Job's complaints, though on a grander scale. God's speech is fraught with power, convincing and convicting. The text does not speak of an occasion when God granted Job a visual encounter, but the experience is so impressive and real that he will later declare, "I had heard of you by the hearing of the ear, but now my eye sees you" (42:5).

## Yahweh's First Speech and Job's Response—38:1–40:5

Job's conversation with Yahweh takes place in two parts, both of them very one-sided because God does most of the talking. There is little for Job to say, and in a way, that's the point. Yahweh's first speech from the whirlwind can be divided into three sections framed by direct challenges to Job. The following outline may help you get a grasp of the larger structure.

Challenge: Yahweh tells Job it is God's place to ask the questions (38:1-3).
    Yahweh questions Job's knowledge of earth and sea (38:4-18).
    Yahweh questions Job's knowledge of weather and the skies (38:19-38).
    Yahweh questions Job's knowledge of animal and bird life (38:39–39:30).
Challenge: Yahweh demands an answer from Job (40:1-2).

Yahweh's opening challenge picks up on Job's frequent allusions to darkness in his previous laments and conversations. From the whirlwind, God's mighty voice asks, "Who is this that darkens counsel by words without knowledge?" (38:2). While Job has raised many complaints and asked many questions, God declares that Job's human limitations have obscured the issues. Job's questions have been based on the same traditional theology defended by his friends, with the only difference being that Job no longer trusts it.

A deep theology of creation is at the heart of the Old Testament's Wisdom literature, and the author's depiction of God pouring out a torrent of questions about creation seems designed to give Job a thorough soaking in it. Apparently, Yahweh wanted Job to gain a larger picture of the universe and the respective place of God and humankind within it. So God turned the tables on Job and declared, "I will question you, and you shall declare to me!" (38:3).

The remainder of chapters 38–39 unleashes a potent flood of questions that flow over Job like a rushing river, pushing him steadily backward with no time to speak the answers he does not have. The initial inundation harks back to God's creation of the earth (38:4-7):

> Where were you when I laid the foundation of the earth?
>     Tell me, if you have understanding.
> Who determined its measurements—surely you know!
>     Or who stretched the line upon it?
> On what were its bases sunk,

or who laid its cornerstone
 when the morning stars sang together
 and all the heavenly beings shouted for joy?

Yahweh's challenge virtually drips with both power and beauty and is staggering in its implications. Could a human really challenge the God who laid the earth's foundations and set the stars in the sky?

Job has no time to catch his breath before Yahweh presses the same line of questioning, expanding it in ever-widening circles, like ripples on a pond. Could Job exercise mastery of the mighty oceans, draw the line of the seashore and demand that it come no further (38:8-11)? Could Job command the morning, tell the sun to rise and thus bring light to the earth (38:12-15)? Could he comprehend the mysteries of the deep and speak with authority about the place of the dead (38:16-17)? The ancients believed all these elements of creation were compassed within "the expanse of the earth" (38:18). Yahweh not only understood them but had created them. Job could only speculate and speak from ignorance.

From the earth and sea, Yahweh's questions rise to examine the heavens. The ancients believed in a multi-storied universe in which the heavens stood above the "firmament," thought to be like a dome over the earth. When rain or snow or hail fell on the earth, the ancients believed that God (or the gods) had opened the windows of heaven and poured the elements through. Speaking in these terms, the author has Yahweh ask Job if he knows how to find the dwelling places of light and darkness, if he has authority to lead them to their respective places (38:19-21).

Storms and weather, so clearly beyond human control, were associated with a variety of gods in the ancient Near East. Images of the Canaanite god Baal, for example, typically portray him with an upraised hand that wields a lightning bolt. The common belief that Baal could control the weather and thus bring good harvests was one reason the Israelites often fell into the idolatrous practices of their Canaanite neighbors.

Job certainly would have professed that Yahweh was in charge of the weather. But does he know anything about the storehouses of snow and hail, or the home of light and the east wind (38:22-24)? God knows where they are and can command them. Can Job? Can Job understand the intricacies of rain and dew and frost and ice (38:25-30)? Can he bind the stars with cosmic chains and lead the constellations on their appointed paths through the heavens (38:31-33)? Can Job count every cloud in the sky? Can he "tilt the waterskins of the heavens" and make it rain (38:34-38)?

Job is quite aware that he can do none of these things. Like a snowman melting in the sun, his sense of self-importance grows smaller with every divine challenge. Before he can confess his impotence, however, Yahweh pours out a new set of challenges. Shifting from the greater to the smaller, God moves from the majesty of the heavens to the marvels of animal life. Like the ringmaster of an impressive circus parade, Yahweh marches representative beasts and birds before Job: lions (38:39-40) and ravens (38:41), mountain goats and wild deer (39:1-4), untamed donkeys (39:5-8) and unbroken oxen (39:9-12). As the parade goes on, Yahweh speaks of the foolishness of ostriches (39:13-18) and the power of horses (39:19-25), of the bloody ways of hawks and eagles (39:26-30)—can Job claim to understand the wonders of God's creation?

No, Job cannot. The text suggests that Yahweh finally pauses with a closing challenge to which Job should respond (40:1-2), but the man on the ash heap knows he is out of his league. There is nothing he can say.

From the whirlwind, Yahweh's challenge is like a roar: "Shall a faultfinder contend with the Almighty? Anyone who argues with God must respond!" Job's response, such as it is, communicates embarrassment and shame. Like someone making the motions of "zipping his lip," Job declares himself to be of small account and unworthy of speech: "I lay my hand on my mouth" (40:4). With this gesture, Job declares that he has already said too much and will say no more (40:5).

## Yahweh's Second Speech and Job's Response—40:6–41:34

The biblical text includes a second overpowering speech that follows a similar pattern, except that Job becomes so demoralized that he does not wait for Yahweh to give a final challenge before responding. The speech begins in the same fashion as the first (compare 38:1, 3 and 40:6-7), insisting that Yahweh will ask the questions and Job must supply the answers.

As the questioning commences, however, Yahweh moves from the creation Job knows (but cannot understand or command) to questions of divine justice and then to mythological creatures, which are equally beyond Job's understanding. While the philosophical issue of theodicy appears to have little in common with the legendary Leviathan and Behemoth, the point is that all are far beyond Job's comprehension or control.

As mentioned previously, some critics observe that the structure and language of this speech appear less artful and more tedious than Yahweh's initial speech. The description of Behemoth, for example, sounds like it could have come from an ancient encyclopedia. Because of the different writing styles, many scholars believe the second speech derives from a second hand.

Here's an outline of Yahweh's second speech:

Challenge: Yahweh will ask, and Job must answer (40:6-7).
    Can Job take control of divine justice? (40:8-14)
    Can a mortal control Behemoth? (40:15-24)
    Can a mortal control Leviathan? (41:1-34 [MT 40:25–41:26])
(No closing challenge)

Have you ever wrongly accused someone of something and experienced an angry response? In this text (40:8-14), Yahweh challenges Job for daring to question divine justice. The voice from the whirlwind blasts Job for persisting in his claim of innocence, even at the cost of implying that God could be in the wrong. The challenge is on target because that is precisely what Job has done, and with good cause: God brought intense suffering to Job's life "for no reason" (2:3). The traditional theology upon which Job had based his understanding of God held that righteous obedience brought divine blessing, while willful rebellion brought punishment. Job knew in his heart that he had not willfully sinned against God. To his mind, then, any break in the divine contract must lie with God.

Does Yahweh's blustery style of question and demand trouble you? There is a sense in which God comes across as a bully. Yahweh asks, "Have you an arm like God, and can you thunder with a voice like his?" (40:9). The implication is that Job's appeal for divine justice is dismissed, not because he is wrong, but because he is a mere human who has no right to challenge God.

The following verses continue the course of intimidation. Yahweh suggests that if Job could clothe himself with the majesty and splendor of divinity, or if he had the ability to look down upon all humans and punish those who are wicked (40:10-13), then there might be a chance "that your own right hand can give you victory" (40:14).

God's next tactic seems a bit odd, for the subject matter shifts from theological debate and turns to nightmarish monsters. It continues the same basic thought, however, because both are impressively beyond Job's comprehension or control. Yahweh calls forth the images of Behemoth (40:15-24) and Leviathan (41:1-34), ancient equivalents of Godzilla and the Loch Ness Monster, legendary creatures that no single human could hope to master.

Behemoth is mentioned only here in the Protestant Bible, though it also appears in the apocryphal book of 2 Esdras (6:49, 51). The name is a direct transliteration of the Hebrew *bĕhēmôt*, a plural form of the word for "cattle." When applied to a singular creature, the form leads to an intensified meaning, something like "super beast."

Yahweh's speech depicts Behemoth as a majestic and powerful land animal. The lengthy description in 40:15-24, written like a textbook entry, does not match any known creature. Some have suggested a hippopotamus or water buffalo as possibilities, but the combination of features in the text does not fully match either one. The animal portrayed sounds like the result of what would happen if someone glimpsed a frightening beast on a dark night, then described it to a string of others who passed the story along with suitable amplifications at each stage, so that the monster became bigger and fiercer with each telling.

While Behemoth roamed the land of ancient nightmares, Leviathan inhabited the sea of bad dreams. Like the sea dragons commonly drawn in the oceans of early maps, Leviathan was imagined as a giant, serpent-like sea creature.

The Hebrews were not the only ancient people who had traditions about such a creature. In Canaanite mythology, Leviathan was called "Lotan" and portrayed as a malevolent monster that had to be subdued by the gods before the earth could be created. The Old Testament likewise implies that Yahweh defeated Leviathan in the course of creation (Ps 74:13-14; Isa 27:1), but also describes Leviathan as a sea beast that God created "for sport" (Ps 104:26). Genesis 1:21 and Psalm 148:7 speak of God's creation of "sea monsters," which may or may not be intended as a reference to Leviathan.

The point, in either case, is not whether Behemoth and Leviathan were inherently good or evil, but that they were powerful and frightful. The beasts needed to be held in check lest they threaten humankind, but Job was clearly not up to the task of catching or restraining them. The rhetorical impact of the speech is that anyone who can't handle giant monsters is simply not on God's level and thus in no position to question God's justice.

Thoroughly disheartened, Job does not wait for Yahweh to issue a closing challenge, but verbally submits to the majesty and might of God. In a brief speech, Job confesses that he has spoken beyond his understanding, acknowledges that he has gained a new appreciation for Yahweh through the impressive personal encounter, and "repents" in dust and ashes (42:1-6).

At first go, reading Job's response can be a bit baffling, because some prominent translations (such as KJV, NAS95, NRSV) don't make it clear that Job has to be quoting God in the opening words of 42:2 and 42:3: "Who is this that hides counsel without knowledge?" (42:2), and "Hear, and I will speak; I will question you, and you declare to me" (42:3). Job is not brashly challenging God with these words, but repeating God's earlier challenge to him in 38:2-3. Thus, it may be helpful to begin both verses with "You asked" and "You said" (as HCSB, NIV, NET), though the words are not in the Hebrew and must be supplied.

Job's response is composed carefully: note that he still admits to no disobedience, only to a lack of appreciation for the immensity of God. Job's key observation is this: "I had heard of you by the hearing of the ear, but now my eye sees you" (42:5). There is no other suggestion that Job literally had seen God with his eyes, but the experience of encountering Yahweh through the whirlwind discourse was so moving and personal that Job could describe his new knowledge of God in visual terms.

**"A Man Should Carry Two Stones in His Pocket"**

Job's stance before God at the end of Job 42:6 invites reflection on the observation of Rabbi Bunam (19th c.): "A man should carry two stones in his pocket. On one should be inscribed, 'I am but dust and ashes.' On the other, 'For my sake the world was created.' And he should use each stone as he needs it."

Cited in R. Gordis, *The Book of God and Man: A Study of Job* (Chicago/London: The University of Chicago Press, 1965), 131.

Job still knows he has committed no sin. Having gained a new awareness of the difference between himself and the great God of the universe, however, he is ready to apologize for failing to appreciate God fully: "therefore I despise myself, and repent in dust and ashes" (42:6).

While Job's response does include an element of self-recrimination, we should note that the verb commonly translated "despise" has no object. Job's primary purpose is to reject his earlier, inadequate understanding of God. Without a stated object, the sense of the verb could be "retract," as understood by NAS95 ("I retract") and HCSB ("I take back [my words].").

This understanding of the word leads to a better understanding of Job's declaration that he will repent in dust and ashes. The word often rendered as "repent" is not the usual word for repentance (*šûḇ*, which literally means "to turn around"), but *nāḥam*, a term that means "to be sorry" or "to console oneself." Job still does not repent of wrongdoing, but expresses sorrow or regret for his former failure to see the bigger picture that Yahweh has shown him.

While "dust and ashes" are typical symbols of grief or repentance, we should not forget that Job retired to the ash heap at 2:8 and has presumably been sitting in dust and ashes throughout the dialogues with his friends and with God. The reference to "dust and ashes," then, may be descriptive of where Job has been all along, rather than a declaration that he will impose new dust and ashes as a sign of repentance. Job's education in suffering began in the dust and ashes of grief and separation; it closes in the dust and ashes of revelation and relationship.

## Job's Intercession—42:7-9

Do you remember the overall structure of Job? The book begins and ends with brief narrative sections that are like bookends to the lengthy poetic dialogues between them. Following Job's impressive encounter with Yahweh's voice from the whirlwind, the poetic dialogues cease, and we come to the closing narrative section. Note the change in style: "And it came about after the LORD had spoken these words to Job, that the LORD said to Eliphaz the Temanite, 'My wrath is kindled against you and against your two friends, because you have not spoken of Me what is right as My servant Job has'" (42:7).

The narrator does not indicate the manner in which Yahweh addressed Eliphaz. A surface reading would suggest that the whirlwind remained present, and perhaps that Job's friends had been listening in all along. The switch from poetry to narrative, however, may suggest that the present story was composed at a different time, and the method of God's speech to Eliphaz is unstated.

Despite the shift in writing style, God's comments to Eliphaz appear to build on the previous conversation between God and Job. Despite the apparently harsh language of Yahweh's stormy speeches to Job, God seems far more pleased by Job's inadequate struggles to understand divine justice than by his friends' smug attempts to defend it.

Note that Eliphaz alone is addressed by name. Bildad and Zophar, presumably, are mentioned only by reference to the Temanite's "two friends." This reinforces earlier hints that Eliphaz was the acknowledged leader of the three inept counselors. Likewise, the complete absence of any reference to Elihu strengthens the probability that he is the product of a different writer who inserted his arguments at a later date.

Eliphaz and his friends had defended both God and the traditional tit-for-tat theology, while Job had raised questions about both. Nevertheless, it is clear that God prefers Job's honest questions to the smugly closed minds of his friends. Yahweh charges, "you have not spoken of me what is right, as my servant Job has" (42:7).

Does this seem odd to you, given the heated nature of God's bombastic speeches to Job? Although Yahweh wanted Job to understand the limits of his knowledge, the clear implication is that God values human honesty, even when it is short on understanding. The three friends had stood firmly on the fundamentals of their faith and dared not question it. They glibly rehashed the conventional theology, but made no apparent effort to understand Job's position or to reconcile it with his protestations of innocence. They could imagine only one solution, that Job must have sinned but refused to admit it. Their spiritual growth was limited by their unwillingness to stretch beyond accepted dogma. Job, however, had spoken the truth. He spoke the truth when affirming his own innocence, and he spoke the truth in declaring that God had not dealt with him rightly—at least within the bounds of his former, limited understanding of God. Job had held to his integrity in the face of an apparently flawed theology, and ultimately he gained a new understanding of divine mystery. Job's friends had been either unwilling or afraid to follow Job into such uncharted theological territory: they spoke what they thought should be said, but it wasn't the truth.

God wanted the three friends to learn the importance of true honesty, however, and demanded that Job's friends learn from the example of their afflicted companion. By whatever means Yahweh spoke to Eliphaz, it apparently made a sufficient impression. He and his friends obeyed God's command to bring seven bulls and seven rams as a whole burnt offering and ask Job—like a priest—to intercede for them, asking forgiveness for their spiritual shortsightedness.

The image of Job as a priest reflects his practice of offering sacrifices in behalf of his children (1:45), so it is not uncharacteristic for Job to be in the position of offering sacrifices as a sin offering for others.

Job's story is portrayed as taking place outside of Israel and before the Israelite institutions of sacrifice were codified, but it was written from the context of people who were familiar with the levitical requirements for sacrifice. Thus, it is worth noting that the number of sacrifices demanded far exceeds the one bull required as a sin offering in Leviticus 4, although that text instructs the priest to dip his fingers in the blood and sprinkle it before the Lord seven times (Lev 4:6, 17). The quantity of sacrifices may be intended as an indication of the severity of the friends' sin in hardening their hearts toward Job and closing their hearts toward any new knowledge about God.

## Job's Restoration—42:10-17

How are we to interpret the closing verses of Job, which recount a time of restoration in which God blesses Job with more than he had to begin with? Throughout the book, Job has questioned the traditional belief that obedience and blessings are necessarily connected. In the end, however, Job's property is not only restored, but doubled. The narrator gives no explanation for this action other than to note that it took place *after* Job had interceded for his friends (42:10, 12), perhaps indicating that Job had both obeyed God and forgiven his friends.

The text does not specifically say that God healed Job's physical ills, though this can be assumed from the statement that "God restored the fortunes of Job" (42:10) and that Job lived a long life (42:16-17). Beyond his health, Job's family is also restored. Not only are ten additional children ultimately born to him, but his brothers, sisters, "and all who had known him before" came to comfort him "for all the evil that the LORD had brought upon him" (42:11).

> **"Job, of All People, Lured God Out of Hiding"**
>
> When the dust settles, Job is strangely pacified. In his last short speech to God, Job admits, "I have spoken of the unspeakable and tried to grasp the infinite. I had heard of you with my ears; but now my eyes have seen you. Therefore, I will be quiet, comforted that I am dust." Why quiet, since he never got an answer, and why comforted that he is dust? Because Job, of all people, lured God out of hiding. He saw God face to face—*panim* to *panim*—and lived to tell the tale.
>
> Barbara Brown Taylor, *When God is Silent* (Cambridge, Boston MS: Cowley Publications, 1998), 70-71.

Do you wonder where Job's family and other friends have been prior to this point? Following Job's tragic losses, sufficient time had passed for Job's three friends to come from their scattered homes, spend seven days sitting in silence, and then enter lengthy dialogues with him. Why did Job's family and other friends wait so long before coming to show sympathy and comfort "for all the evil that the LORD had brought upon him" and to aid him by bringing "a piece of money and a gold ring"?

The narrator does not say, though we may note that the arrival of other comforters any earlier in the story would have interrupted the narrative flow. Their arrival at the end of the story serves the narrator's purpose of showing how God restored blessings upon Job after he had proven faithful, and it also contrasts the effective consolation of Job's family with the clumsy efforts of his friends.

You may also wonder why Job's wife is not mentioned in the account of Job's restoration. The narrator indicates that seven sons and three daughters are restored to Job, but offers no details about their births or their mother. This piques our curiosity: did Job's wife, if we may assume that she was the mother of the first ten children, bear ten more? Since Job's wife is described in unflattering terms in 2:9-10 and is not mentioned here, should we imagine that Job has a new wife? Or, in the fashion of other ancient patriarchs, might he have had multiple wives or concubines all along? While these questions leave us wondering, they do not concern the narrator, whose primary purpose is to catalog the divine blessings that indicate God's renewed favor toward Job.

Surprisingly, the author of the epilogue singles out Job's daughters for special mention: of all Job's family members, only they are named. The fact that the narrator records the daughters' names is more significant than the meaning of the names, but for the record, "Jemimah" means "dove"; "Keziah" is the word for cassia, a type of cinnamon; and "Keren-Happuch" means something like "mascara box."

We must note that the narrator not only names Job's daughters, but praises them as the most beautiful women in the land. Recall that Job had been described as the greatest man in the East (1:3); now his daughters are depicted as the most beautiful.

As if the distinctives of name and beauty were not enough to set the daughters apart, the narrator says something even more astounding: Job gave his daughters a share of his newly-enlarged inheritance along with their brothers (42:13-15). Ordinarily, only sons inherited, with the oldest son receiving the largest share. Now the daughters are included, too.

We noted in the first session that the story of Job began in fairy-tale style: "There once was a man . . . ." Thus, we should not be surprised to find that it concludes with a "happily ever after" ending—the text concludes by saying Job lived another 140 years, seeing children to the fourth generation after him, and died "old and full of days" (42:16-17).

## THEOLOGICAL THEMES

How are we to understand these last chapters, including God's answer to Job—if it really is an answer? Job had longed for some explanation from God, but what he got was neither what he expected nor what we might anticipate.

In a sense, the very expectation that Yahweh would offer a defense to Job creates an unlikely scenario that puts God in the position of arguing on a human level. Some issues may simply be beyond human understanding: "When the question has to do with innocent suffering, '*no* answer' may be *the* answer we need to hear from God, even if it is difficult to accept."[1]

How are we to understand God's response to Job, and how does it inform our own times of suffering? Many have sought to comprehend God's reply, and none can claim to have the final answer. Perhaps the best we can do is to observe that, in the end, God's wisdom and justice simply transcend human comprehension. Consider this inadequate example: picture a four-year-old boy who complains to his mother when things don't go his way. Little Joe Bob may be distraught and may have a clear understanding of why he feels wronged, but he is simply incapable of seeing the situation as his mother does. Her experience, wisdom, and adult perspective enable her to see a much larger picture than the child can see. Job has a clear idea about what he believes is right and wrong, but he simply cannot see what God can see.

A second major issue for interpreters is the meaning of Job's restoration. Does the return of divine blessing—doubled, even—suggest a return to the status quo of *quid pro quo*? That is not necessarily the case. Note that God does not just restore Job's fortunes, but restores them twofold. Rising from the point of death, Job is also given an additional 140 years of life—double the amount expected in Psalm 90:10. These doubled restorations of property and life may reflect the regulations found in Exodus 22 that require thieves who steal another's animals to repay two to four times as much as they took. God had allowed the accuser to take all that Job owned for "no reason." Perhaps the author intends to suggest that God had allowed Job's goods to be stolen and was paying retribution for the loss. From this perspective, Job's restoration would be a repayment of God's debt rather than a divine reward for Job's obedience, a setting that would affirm the traditional theology.

Another suggestion that things have changed is found in the emphasis given to Job's daughters: not only are they the only members of Job's family to be named, but the text points out that Job gives them as well as their brothers an inheritance. Patriarchal conventions called for daughters to inherit only if there were no sons (Num 27:1-11). Perhaps Job's experience gave new shape to his understanding of justice. He had been the victim of an injustice, and it may be that the social custom of dividing one's estate between sons but not daughters no longer seemed fair or appropriate to him.

Thus, a quick look at the surface might lead us to assume that the closing chapter reaffirms the tit-for-tat theology that Job has challenged throughout the book, but a closer inspection suggests that the "greatest man of the East" has grown even greater in his understanding of the mysteries of God and has much to teach us.

## LITERARY THEMES

We have noted that Job's dialogue with God, as with his friends, is presented in poetry. There are times when poetry can speak to an issue more clearly than narrative. One of my favorite commentaries on Job is found in the poetry of Robert Frost. In a long, rambling poem called "A Masque of Reason," Frost imagines that Job is in heaven and having a conversation with the Lord, who reminisces about the trials Job endured.[2]

As Frost tells it, Job has just asked God a question about heaven, and this is how God responds:

Yes, by and by. But first a larger matter.
I've had you on my mind a thousand years
To thank you someday for the way you helped me
Establish once for all the principle
There's no connection a man can reason out
Between his just desserts and what he gets.
Virtue may fail and wickedness succeed.
'Twas a great demonstration we put on . . .

But it was of the essence of the trial
You shouldn't understand it at the time.
It had to seem unmeaning to have meaning.
And it came out all right. I have no doubt
You realize by now the part you played
To stultify the Deuteronomist
And change the tenor of religious thought.
My thanks are to you for releasing me
From moral bondage to the human race . . .
I had to prosper good and punish evil.
You changed all that. You set me free to reign.

Frost's poetry captures an important key to understanding the story of Job: both Job and his friends struggled with an inadequate view of God that limited divine sovereignty to a rigid system of rewards and punishments. Job learns that God is far bigger than any theological box that humans can comprehend.

## SPIRITUALITY AND MINISTRY THEMES

How does our interaction with Job affect our own struggle to understand the things that happen to us and the question of whether God is responsible? When Job finally found peace with God and with himself, it was not because he got his questions answered or because his wealth was restored and he had more children, but because he caught a vision of God's greatness that helped him break out of his old preconceptions and see God in a new way.

The truth is, there is a real sense in which Job never did get an answer to his questions. What he got was *God*, and that was what he needed most. Job found a God who is bigger than he had ever imagined, a God who must be free of human preconceptions about what God *must* do. Job paid a terrible price for the lesson, but he learned, in essence, that God could not be subject to human demands and still be God.

Job's experience challenges us to ask whether we also can accept a God whose behavior is not subject to our fixed ideas about how God must behave.

# STUDY QUESTIONS

1. In seeking to understand Job's encounter with God, what do you think of this quotation from M. Tzevat? "The god who speaks to man in the book of Job is neither just nor unjust. He is God."[3]

2. How are we to understand God's answer to Job—if it really is an answer? How do you understand it? Is it fruitless for humans to call divine justice into question?

3. How does Job's restoration affect the story? Does it make it easier or more difficult to interpret? Does it reinforce the same theology Job's friends had declared, or call it into question?

# QUESTIONS FOR PERSONAL REFLECTION

1. Has your understanding of Job changed as a result of this study? If so, how?

2. Has your personal theology or understanding of God been challenged as a result of this study? If so, how?

3. Do you have any new insights or understanding about suffering as a result of this study? Explain.

4. What is the most important insight you will carry with you from this study?

# NOTES

[1] Samuel Balentine, *Job*, Smyth & Helwys Bible Commentary (Macon GA: Smyth & Helwys, 2006), 628.

[2] Robert Frost, "A Masque of Reason," in Edward Connery Lathan, ed., *The Poetry of Robert Frost* (New York: Holt, Rinehart and Winston, 1969), 473-90.

[3] M. Tzevat, in "The Meaning of the Book of Job," *Hebrew Union College Annual* 37 (1966): 105.

# GLOSSARY OF TERMS

**aphorism**—A traditional saying intended to pass on wisdom. For example, "Early to bed and early to rise makes a man healthy and wealthy and wise."

**Apocrypha**—Ancient writings, mostly written between Old and New Testament times, that are accepted as Scripture by most Catholics but not by most Protestants.

**Behemoth**—An unidentifiable but frightening land-based "superbeast" described in Job 40:15-24.

**canon**—The accepted corpus of biblical books. Books that are not considered a part of the Bible are called extra-canonical.

**curse**—A wish for something bad to befall a person or thing. In ancient times, many believed that uttering the wish would set the events into motion.

**Deuteronomistic**—Refers to writings or beliefs contained in the book of Deuteronomy, which taught that obedience to God led to blessings, while the rebellious would be cursed.

**didactic**—Intended for teaching purposes.

**epilogue**—A literary term describing the concluding section of a book.

**exile**—In the Old Testament, a term referring to the time spent by Israel and Judah in captivity. Israel was conquered by the Assyrians about 721 BC. Judah was conquered by the Babylonians in 593 and 582 BC. The exile officially ended about 538 BC, when Cyrus the Persian conquered Babylon and began allowing Hebrews to return to Jerusalem and the surrounding areas.

**Leviathan**—A giant, fearsome, fire-breathing sea serpent described in Job 41:1-34. In Canaanite mythology, Leviathan was called "Lotan."

**levitical**—Pertaining to the priestly laws or practices of the ancient Hebrews, most of which are found in the book of Leviticus.

**oath**—In the Old Testament, an oath consisted of a promise that was reinforced by a curse against oneself if the oath-maker failed to fulfill the promise.

**parallelism**—A term used to describe the central characteristic of Hebrew poetry, in which two or more lines complement each other. "Synonymous parallelism" pairs two lines that say the same thing in different words. With "antithetical parallelism," two lines make the same point by saying it in opposite ways. In "synthetic" or "formal" parallelism, the thought spoken in the first line of a unit is amplified or advanced in the following line (or lines), but not repeated.

**post-exilic**—The period after the exile (see above) when Israelites were allowed to return to Jerusalem and the surrounding areas.

**prologue**—A literary term describing the introductory part of a longer work.

**Sheol**—In Hebrew thought, the land of the dead, where all people were thought to continue a shadowy underground existence after death.

**theodicy**—An attempt to explain and justify the presumed acts of God, usually with reference to defending God's goodness despite the presence of evil.

**theology**—Literally, "the study of God." Theology attempts to understand the nature and actions of God.

**Wisdom literature**—Collections of proverbs or extended writings designed to pass on wisdom from one generation to the next, probably used in school settings. In the Bible, the books of Proverbs, Job, and Ecclesiastes are considered to be Wisdom literature.

**Yahweh**—The personal name for God revealed in the Old Testament. Only the consonants *yhwh* were written, so the pronunciation is uncertain. Most scholars believe "Yahweh," which could also mean "he who causes to be," is the most likely pronunciation.

www.ingramcontent.com/pod-product-compliance
Lightning Source LLC
Chambersburg PA
CBHW060533030426
42337CB00021B/4247